DINOSAURS

Written by Sarah Eason
Illustrated by James Field

ARMADILLO

This edition is published by Armadillo,
an imprint of Anness Publishing Ltd,
108 Great Russell Street, London WC1B 3NA;
info@anness.com

www.armadillobooks.co.uk; www.annesspublishing.com;
twitter: @Anness_Books

If you like the images in this book and would like to
investigate using them for publishing, promotions or
advertising, please visit www.practicalpictures.com
for more information.

Publisher: Joanna Lorenz
Project Manager: Helen Parker
Editor: Steve Parker
Consultant: James Field
Indexer: Jane Parker
Design: Trait Design
Production Controller: Ben Worley

PUBLISHER'S NOTE
Although the advice and information in this book are
believed to be accurate and true at the time of going
to press, neither the authors nor the publisher can
accept any legal responsibility or liability for any errors
or omissions that may have been made.

Manufacturer: Anness Publishing Ltd,
108 Great Russell Street, London WC1B 3NA, England
For Product Tracking go to:
www.annesspublishing.com/tracking
Batch: 7002-24119-1127

Contents

Understanding Dinosaurs

All dinosaurs had tails. Many used their tails to balance their bodies when standing or running on their hind legs.

Dinosaurs laid eggs. Some dinosaurs even built nests and may have guarded their young.

Some plant-eating dinosaurs swallowed smooth stones to help grind up the food in their stomachs. These are called gastroliths.

Large plant-eaters may have eaten more than 200kg (450lb) of food each day!

Some dinosaurs were as long and as heavy as the biggest whales of today. Others were as small as a chicken.

The largest dinosaurs were the sauropods. Some of these may have measured a staggering 35m (115ft) long and weighed more than 100 tons!

Diplodocus, a huge sauropod dinosaur

Rhamphorhynchus, a pterosaur

Dinosaurs were probably the most successful animals that ever lived on Earth. They dominated the planet for around 135 million years. Most scientists believe that dinosaurs were members of the large animal group called reptiles, which includes lizards, crocodiles, snakes, turtles and tortoises. In fact 'dinosaur' means 'terrible lizard'. The skeleton of a dinosaur closely resembles the bones of today's reptiles, especially the crocodiles. Dinosaurs also had thick leathery skin covered with scales, for protection and to prevent them from losing moisture in hot weather.

Stegosaurus, a plated dinosaur

All dinosaurs lived on land. But other reptiles of their time flew in the sky, and yet others swam in the oceans. We can tell that dinosaurs lived on land by studying the structure of their bodies. Like our own legs, the legs of a dinosaur were straight and positioned underneath the body, not sprawling to the sides, as in a lizard.

dactylus, rosaur

Dinosaurs are divided into two groups, saurischians and ornithischians. The differences are based on the structure of their hip bones, called the pelvis. Saurischians included all meat-eating dinosaurs, from huge *Tyrannosaurus* to tiny *Compsognathus*, as well as the mainly large plant-eating dinosaurs called sauropods.

All ornithischians were plant-eaters. These dinosaurs also had an extra toothless bone at the front of their jaws, which in some cases was covered by a horny beak. They used this beak for snipping and cropping leaves and other plant parts.

The largest meat-eating dinosaurs, like Tyrannosaurus, were the biggest hunting animals ever to live on land. They used their huge jaws and razor-sharp teeth to kill their prey, then rip it apart. Or they were scavengers, feasting on the bodies of other dinosaurs which had died from disease or injury.

Tyrannosaurus had more than 50 curved, blade-like teeth

Troodon, a small and agile meat-eating dinosaur

5

Discovering Dinosaurs

Dinosaur Facts

Megalosaurus was one of the first dinosaurs to be named, in 1824 by William Buckland.

Dinosaur fossils have been found on every continent in the world, even Antarctica.

Giant bird-like footprints found in Connecticut Valley, USA in the early 1800s were thought to belong to ancient birds. They were recognized as dinosaur footprints in the 1870s.

The fossils of small meat-eating dinosaurs and prehistoric birds are very similar. There has often been confusion over which is which.

Dinosaurs have fascinated people ever since they became known from their fossil remains. In AD 300 Chinese scholar Chang Qu discovered bones in Sichuan province which he said came from a giant dragon. From his description of the bones, scientists later identified the creature as a dinosaur. Native American Indians unearthed huge bones which they believed belonged to a giant bison, and they carried these into battle, believing they would bring good luck. The bones they discovered were probably those of dinosaurs.

When dinosaur bones were first discovered in China they were thought to be the remains of giant dragons!

William Buckland, the first Professor of Geology at Oxford University

Native Americans thought that dinosaur fossils might have come from giant bison.

In 1824 the first dinosaur was named by an eccentric English vicar named William Buckland. He discovered the fossil jaw of the giant meat-eater *Megalosaurus*. At the time the term 'dinosaur' did not exist, but Buckland recognized the remains as being from a strange type of giant animal, and gave them a name meaning 'big lizard'. This was the first official recording of a dinosaur.

A year later, an English country doctor named Gideon Mantell published his drawings and description of what he thought was a giant lizard, which he named *Iguanodon*. Mantell was a doctor, fossil collector and geologist, and he saw the similarity between the fossil teeth and those of the much smaller iguana lizard.

The discoveries of men like Buckland and Mantell shocked and amazed scientists and ordinary people alike. At the time, people believed that the only creatures alive on Earth before human beings were primitive forms of the animals they saw about them. The suggestion that giant, lizard-like creatures had stalked the Earth many millions of years before humans first appeared seemed unthinkable.

In the years that followed, the fascination with dinosaurs grew. More and more fossils were found and recorded. After the naming of both *Megalosaurus* and *Iguanodon*, and another dinosaur, the armoured plant-eater *Hylaeosaurus*, palaeontologist (fossil expert) Richard Owen at last gave

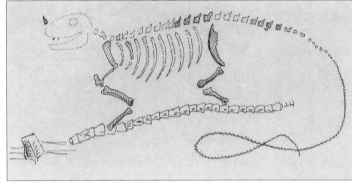

Gideon Mantell

these creatures the name by which we know them today. In 1841 he invented the term for the group, Dinosauria, which means 'terrible lizard'.

Since 1825, thousands of dinosaur skeletons have been discovered and reconstructed.

From Europe to North and South America, Asia, Africa, Australia and beyond, fossilized remains of dinosaurs and their eggs have helped us to build a picture of these incredible creatures.

Mantell published his ideas about the fossils he had found, and a sketch of the reconstructed skeleton, in 1825. He described an enormous, plant-eating creature whose teeth were similar to those of the American iguana lizard. Mantell named the beast Iguanodon, 'iguana tooth'. At the time, the name 'dinosaur' did not exist.

The fossil jawbone and teeth below, discovered by William Buckland, once belonged to the huge meat-eating dinosaur Megalosaurus. It was the first fossil specimen of a dinosaur to be given a formal scientific name, meaning simply 'big lizard'.

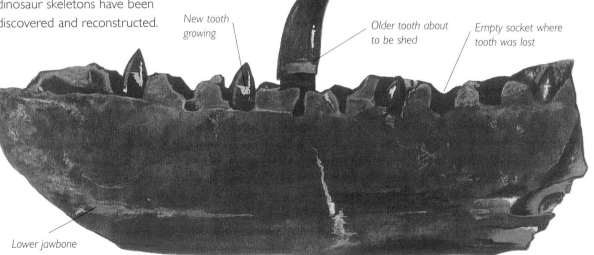

New tooth growing

Older tooth about to be shed

Empty socket where tooth was lost

Lower jawbone

The World the Dinosaurs Knew

Eoraptor, a very early meat-eating dinosaur

The Earth changes constantly. Its land masses shift and move, and molten rock from the Earth's core rises to the surface, creating new land or ocean floor. As a result, the Earth today is a very different planet from the one inhabited by dinosaurs.

Megazostrodon, an early mammal

Millions of years ago, the world was much warmer, with no ice caps near the North and South Poles. This climate allowed animal and plant life to flourish worldwide, providing an environment in which many species of dinosaur thrived.

Archaeopteryx, the first known bird

The dinosaurs lived during three spans or periods of geological time – Triassic, Jurassic and Cretaceous. During the Triassic period, all land on Earth was joined together in one giant continent called Pangaea.

Laurasia

North America

Europe

Africa

Gondwanaland

South America

Massospondylus, one of the first large dinosaurs

8

Dimorphodon, a pterosaur

Asia

South-East Asia

Tethys Sea

dia

rctica   Australia

Because Earth was one large land mass, few places were near the sea, resulting in a very dry climate in the interior. The Jurassic period saw the break-up of the single land mass into two separate

Allosaurus, a huge Jurassic meat-eater

continents. Seas spread across parts of the land, and the continents began to drift into the positions we know today.

Archaeopteryx, which had a skeleton almost identical to some small dinosaurs. The Jurassic is also famous for its terrifying meat-eaters, such as *Allosaurus* and *Ceratosaurus*.

Plant and tree life also changed. In the Jurassic period, many types of trees such as monkey-puzzles and conifers thrived. In the Cretaceous the first flowers and blossom trees appeared near the equator, and spread worldwide.

As the world became wetter, many reptiles adapted to sea life. During the Jurassic and Cretaceous periods, marine (sea-living) types flourished. Elasmosaurus was a plesiosaur, with a neck 5m (16ft) long!

During the Jurassic period, the single land mass called Pangaea began to split into two supercontinents, known as Laurasia and Gondwanaland.

Struthiomimus, a Cretaceous 'ostrich-dinosaur'

During the Jurassic and Cretaceous periods, the climate became gradually cooler and damper. The first birds appeared, joining flying reptiles called pterosaurs. Birds probably developed from dinosaurs – the oldest is

Corythosaurus, a Cretaceous plant-eating dinosaur

Dinosaur Bodies

Sauropods like Brachiosaurus had a huge muscular stomach called a gizzard. Here large amounts of vegetation were pounded into a paste. The food was then passed to the intestines, a long string of tubes where the nutrients were absorbed.

Gullet

Lung

Intestines

Kidney

Windpipe

Heart

Female sex organs

Liver

Gizzard

Dinosaur Facts

The small meat-eater Troodon had a brain that was as large as a bird's brain — and birds like parrots are quite clever!

Iguanodon had huge sheets of muscle on its legs, which helped it to run at speed for short distances.

Most dinosaurs had eyes that were set at the sides of their head. This helped them to see all around them without moving their heads.

Heavy dinosaurs had huge, thick legs, like an elephant's limbs, to support their weight. Lighter dinosaurs had hollow, thin bones.

Some plant-eating dinosaurs swallowed stones called gastroliths to help crush vegetation inside their stomachs. Gastroliths smoothed by this rubbing are often found near the skeletons of large plant-eaters like the sauropods.

The soft parts of dinosaur bodies rotted away soon after death, or were eaten by scavengers. Unlike the hard parts such as bones, teeth, claws and horns, they were not preserved as fossils. However, we can make a reasonable guess at the internal structure of a dinosaur, using clues from today's animals, especially reptiles. Within the skeleton lay various internal organs.

Plateosaurus had a long light skull and small, diamond-shaped teeth. This dinosaur, a prosauropod, fed mainly on tree leaves and other vegetation.

DINOSAUR BRAINS

Dinosaur brain size varied from species to species. Some, like *Stegosaurus*, had very small brains – only the size of a walnut, and 1/20,000th the size of the whole body. Others, like *Troodon*, had brains that were relatively large, 1/200th the size of the body.

Stegosaurus

Brain

Brain

Troodon (back) compared to a gamebird (front)

Saurischian dinosaurs (left, above) had lizard-like hip bones in which the pubis bone faced forwards. Ornithischians (left, below) had a bird-like hip design in which the pubis faced backwards.

Ilium

Pubis *Ischium*

Ilium

Ischium

Pubis

These included the heart, lungs, liver and intestines. The intestines probably varied depending on whether the dinosaur was a plant- or meat-eater. Meat-eaters would have quite short digestive canals, but plant-eaters probably had a long and complex system, which could break down vegetation. Teeth also varied greatly. Plant-eaters had large, flat teeth or small

peg-like teeth, which were used to crop, rake up or grind leaves and other vegetation.

Meat-eaters had sharp, dagger-like teeth, to tear into and rip out flesh. In all dinosaurs, old or broken teeth were replaced by new ones.

Most dinosaurs had relatively small brains for their body size. Huge meat-eaters like

Tyrannosaurus had dagger-like teeth white sharp edges. They curved backwards to stop struggling brey from escaping.

Tyrannosaurus had a brain that would have been skilled at controlling the movements of its limbs, but the cerebrum (thinking part of the brain) was very small. The brain of a giant sauropod was tiny compared to the rest of its body. Some very small dinosaurs had highly developed brains, however, which were as complicated as a bird's brain.

It is thought that dinosaurs may have used various body-heating systems. Some may have maintained a constant body temperature, like birds and mammals. Others may have absorbed heat from the sun's rays during the day, and stored it in their massive bodies to keep them warm during the night.

Tyrannosaurus had razor-sharp teeth up to 18cm (7in) long – that's as long as a large kitchen knife!

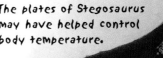

The plates of Stegosaurus may have helped control body temperature.

How Dinosaurs Moved

The ability of dinosaurs to stand on straight, upright legs gave enormous freedom of movement. It was partly this mobility that made the dinosaurs such a huge success. From giant plant-eaters and meat-eaters to tiny scavengers, the upright position made a huge difference to survival. The hips, in particular, were very strong and allowed them to walk in an upright position. In most dinosaurs the long, flexible tail helped to balance the weight over the hips. This combination of stability and agility made dinosaurs one of the most successful creatures ever to exist on land. They contrasted greatly with most other reptiles, which had more of a sprawling posture. All four legs are splayed either side of the body with bent 'elbows' and 'knees'. This posture is very restrictive and energy-consuming, and makes it difficult to walk and run continuously over long distances. Dinosaurs could walk and run faster and for longer periods of time.

Dinosaur Facts

Large sauropods like Diplodocus and Brachiosaurus kept their tails off the ground as they moved.

Fossilized trackways, or trails of footprints, show how dinosaurs moved. They can tell us how fast dinosaurs walked and ran, and whether on two legs or four.

Diplodocus had three sharp-clawed inner toes on its back feet. These probably helped to stop it from slipping as it walked or reached up on its hind legs.

The ostrich-dinosaur Gallimimus was a very fast runner, probably racing along at speeds of 65km (40 miles) per hour!

Diplodocus

Camptosaurus

Lesothosaurus

Enormous meat-eaters like *Tyrannosaurus* could perhaps run as fast as most prey. Some estimates put this predator's sprinting speed at about 10km (6 miles) per hour. Other estimates, based on the size of the leg muscles, are three times faster! This large meat-eater's ability to stand on two legs gave a lethal combination of power and speed.

Some dinosaurs could move either on two legs (bipedally), or on all four (quadrupedally). They could stand up on two legs and use their front feet as hands, to grip food or fight. Or they could move around on all four legs. *Iguanodon* could probably do this, moving around on four or two legs. It had unusually powerful arms, which helped to carry its huge weight while walking on all fours. On its hand, the thumb had a long, bony spike. When this dinosaur raised itself up on to two legs, it could use this spiked thumb as a weapon to stab enemies, or to pull food from trees.

The tracks of a lizard show how the feet are wider apart than the narrower foot-span of a dinosaur. Evidence such as this shows that dinosaurs walked in an upright position.

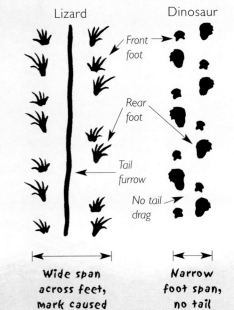

Lizard   Dinosaur

Front foot

Rear foot

Tail furrow

No tail drag

Wide span across feet, mark caused by tail

Narrow foot span, no tail mark

Parasaurolophus

Plateosaurus

Allosaurus

Deinonychus

Stegosaurus

HOW ANIMALS STAND AND WALK

There are three ways in which four-legged animals walk. Lizards crawl along the ground, with all four legs splayed out from their bodies. Crocodiles walk in a slightly more upright position, with straighter legs to hold their bodies farther off the ground. Unlike any other reptile before or since, dinosaurs walked fully upright, with straight legs tucked beneath their bodies.

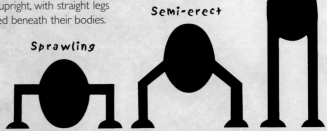

Fully erect

Semi-erect

Sprawling

Compsognathus

Big and Little Dinosaurs

Mention the word 'dinosaur' and most people think of huge, towering creatures. However, the prehistoric age was also filled with smaller dinosaurs which, despite their size, flourished in an environment teeming with gigantic plant-eaters and monstrous hunters. The sauropods were the largest of all dinosaurs, even towering over huge meat-eaters such as *Tyrannosaurus* and *Allosaurus*.

One of the tallest sauropods, *Brachiosaurus*, would have been able to reach into the highest trees to feed on their leaves, using its enormously long neck and standing tall on its giraffe-like front legs. While the huge sauropods plodded across the prehistoric landscape, smaller dinosaurs relied upon their light, slight bodies for speed. One plant-eater, *Hypsilophodon*, had a body that stood only 1.5m (5ft) tall. Its length from nose to tail was about 2m (7ft), compared to the enormous 27m (88ft) long *Diplodocus*. Built like the reptile version of a gazelle, *Hypsilophodon*'s entire body was finely honed into the smallest size and slimmest shape possible, allowing it to sprint across the landscape if under attack. With no other way of defending itself, *Hypsilophodon* must have relied upon its tiny, slight build and darting speed to hide in the undergrowth.

Dinosaur Facts

Brachiosaurus was as tall as a four-floor building!

Compsognathus was the weight of a domestic cat!

Seismosaurus is one of the largest dinosaur skeletons found to date. The shoulder blade alone of this enormous dinosaur is much taller than a fully-grown man.

The thigh bone of Brachiosaurus measures 2m (6½ft) – that's much taller than you!

Argentinosaurus was a huge sauropod that weighed as much as 20 elephants!

Compsognathus

14

Of the well-known dinosaurs, *Compsognathus* was the smallest. Just the size of a chicken, this tiny meat-eater relied upon its agile body and sharp senses for survival. Indeed *Compsognathus* was built more like a bird than a reptile, with a narrow, pointed head, a small body and a surprisingly long tail, which it used for balance as it stood, walked and ran on its two hind legs. *Compsognathus* weighed just 3kg (6½lb), as light as a feather compared to the enormous 50-ton bulk of *Brachiosaurus*!

Tyrannosaurus

Brachiosaurus was once thought to be the largest sauropod. But recent fossil discoveries, such as Seismosaurus and Argentinosaurus, show that some sauropods may have been even larger.

One early discovery that may signify the biggest dinosaur ever recorded, was found in 1878 by Edward Cope. He discovered a 1.5m (5ft) section of vertebrae (backbone) in Colorado, USA. Although the further bones of the creature were never found, it was still possible to work out how large the dinosaur may have been – a staggering 60m (200ft) long and weighing 150 tons! If such calculations are correct, this single fossil bone could represent the largest dinosaur that ever lived.

Edward Drinker Cope was an American fossil-hunter. Working against his chief rival, Othniel Charles Marsh, he discovered many important dinosaur remains in North America during the 1870s-90s, including Allosaurus, Apatosaurus, Diplodocus and Stegosaurus.

Diplodocus

Hypsilophodon

HEIGHT AND WEIGHT

Brachiosaurus is still one of the largest dinosaurs known from fairly complete fossil remains, and *Diplodocus* one of the longest. However, limited remains of other dinosaurs show that they may have been even larger. *Argentinosaurus* could have reached 30m (100ft) in length and 100 tons in weight.

Argentinosaurus　*Brachiosaurus*

Seismosaurus

Great Meat-eaters

The age of the dinosaurs produced some of the most terrifying meat-eating creatures on Earth. From huge *Tyrannosaurus* and *Allosaurus* to the fierce, deadly, group-hunting *Velociraptor*, these creatures were finely tuned killing machines, programmed to hunt. Unlike plant-eating dinosaurs, which could regularly feed from the surrounding vegetation, meat-eaters had to catch their food. Like the great animal hunters of today, meat-eating dinosaurs probably made short, energetic hunts for prey and then rested until they needed to feed again. Large, predatory (hunting) dinosaurs like *Allosaurus* may have stalked their prey, following groups of plant-eaters and then charging, or ambushing them for the kill. Although equipped to hunt, these huge dinosaurs had other ways of finding a meal.

Dinosaur Facts

The fossil remains of meat-eating dinosaurs have been found on every continent in the world, even Antarctica!

Allosaurus was the largest land predator of the Late Jurassic period. It was 11m (36ft) long, stood up to 4.5m (15ft) tall, and weighed 2 tons.

In the 1990s the fossils of a meat-eater, which was even bigger than Tyrannosaurus, were found in South America. Giganotosaurus was probably 15m (50ft) long and weighed more than 8 tons.

Pubis part of hip bone

Caudal vertebrae of tail

Chevron extensions of tail bones

Femur (thigh bone)

Tibia and fibula (shin bones)

Ankle joint

3 walking toes with sharp claws

SKELETON OF ALLOSAURUS

RECONSTRUCTION OF ALLOSAURUS

Eye socket (orbit)

Nares (opening for nostril)

Brain case (cranium)

Jaw joint

Lower jaw (mandible)

New tooth growing

Older tooth

SKULL OF ALLOSAURUS

The jaws of Allosaurus contained almost 60 saw-edged, razor-sharp teeth, to kill and tear apart its prey.

Fleeing herd
of Diplodocus

Hungry Allosaurus may have
hunted in pairs or small
groups to bring down their
prey. Allosaurus would
have picked off any
weak, sick or elderly
dinosaurs from a herd
of plant-eaters like
Diplodocus.

Ornitholestes
catching a
lizard

Ceratosaurus

Nose horn

Allosaurus

Rather than waste their
energy chasing after living
prey, they may have stolen the
meals of smaller meat-eaters.
Or they may have fed off the
leftovers of another large
dinosaur's dinner, if the
opportunity arose.

Some scientists believe that
huge meat-eaters like
Tyrannosaurus and Allosaurus
may have survived by
scavenging – eating already-
dead animals. Today's great
hunters, such as lions and
tigers, accept a dead carcass as
a meal, especially when food is
generally in short supply. Or
they pick off the very young,
very old, sick and infirm as
easy targets.

A typical
hunt by a
meat-eater like
Allosaurus
would begin
by tracking a
herd of plant-
eaters. The
herbivores were
often armoured or
able to outrun a large
meat-eater, or they could use
their huge bulk or whiplash
tails, so they were by no
means an easy target. Sick,
young or elderly dinosaurs
would have been most at risk
and certainly easier to attack
than healthy adults. Perhaps
Allosaurus would have been
able to sense which dinosaur
was most vulnerable, and then

single it out from the herd.
Some large meat-eaters may
have stalked their prey for
many hours, hiding from sight
and perhaps rushing out from
cover. Great care would have
been taken to avoid detection.
If any of the herd caught sight,
scent or sound of a predator,
it would have immediately

alerted the group to
danger. The herd would
then run away or possibly
form a protective ring around
younger members, shielding
them from attack.

A World of Carnivores

Although giants such as *Tyrannosaurus* and *Allosaurus* stand out as the most awesome meat-eaters of the dinosaur age, there were also a number of smaller, less famous carnivores that were just as deadly to their smaller prey. Of these

smaller hunters, *Deinonychus* and *Velociraptor* are perhaps the most spine-chilling. These ferocious dinosaurs, known as raptors, would probably hunt in small groups, tracking down and then attacking their prey in a synchronized ambush.

The body structure of a raptor was slight, with light, fine bones and long legs, but powerful muscles. A long, stiff tail at the rear helped the

hunters to balance as they moved. Jaws with razor-sharp teeth, and slicing claws on the hand and feet, made them especially fearsome killers.

The name *Deinonychus* means 'terrible claw'. This raptor could run very fast, and leap upon its victim at speed and with great agility. *Deinonychus* would have prowled the landscape in small packs, searching

for food. Through combined attack, the pack would be able to kill a dinosaur much larger than themselves.

Dinosaur Facts

The first Deinonychus skeleton was found in the USA in 1964 by John Ostrom of Yale University, USA.

Deinonychus was only the length of a small car and the weight of an average human being.

Coelophysis means 'hollow form'. This dinosaur was named from its light, hollow bones and bird-like shape.

Raptors like Deinonychus and Velociraptor probably hunted in packs to bring down their prey.

Claw in resting position, held off ground for walking

Claw swings around in arc for attack

Claw finishes slashing arc

Point of claw rips flesh

The second toe of Deinonychus had a huge, curved claw that could swivel through a half-circle in a flash, to slice through a victim's flesh like a knife.

Once a suitable meal, such as a plant-eating *Tenontosaurus*, had been identified, the group attacked with force. Racing forwards, the hunters would leap on to the plant-eater, cutting at its flesh with their razor-sharp claws. The powerful jaws of the *Deinonychus* could bite into the flesh of its victim, tearing through skin and muscle with ease. A sizeable plant-eater like *Tenontosaurus* may have been able to put up a fight, but the sheer force of the group would eventually be too much for the victim, and death through shock and loss of blood would result.

However, not all meat-eaters hunted large prey. Smaller dinosaurs fed on lizards, mammals, insects, worms and any other small creatures that were readily available.

Coelophysis was an agile hunter. This smallish, very slim, lightweight dinosaur lived more than 200 million years ago. It probably fed on insects, lizards and small mammals, but may also have been a cannibal, eating its own kind – especially babies just hatched from their eggs in the nest. Some reptiles today do this.

Hatchlings emerge

Deinonychus was a medium-sized, powerful killer. It could run at speed and leap to launch an attack on victims such as Tenontosaurus.

The body build and proportions of Velociraptor, along with details of its fossil bones, suggest to some experts that this dinosaur was warm-blooded. So it may have had fluffy, downy feathers or fur to keep itself warm.

Long, stiff, balancing tail

Long, light skull

Flexible neck

Agile, lightly-built body

Small forearms

Three large-clawed fingers

Sickle claw

19

Under Attack

An attack by a predatory meat-eater such as *Allosaurus* would have begun by either tracking a sick, young or old dinosaur among a herd of plant-eaters, such as *Diplodocus* or *Camptosaurus*, or by lying in wait and then ambushing the prey.

Once the chosen victim had become separated from the group, *Allosaurus* would charge with surprising speed. This huge meat-eater could run at perhaps more than 30km (18 miles) per hour for short distances. The startled plant-eater may have tried to rejoin its herd, but other *Allosaurus* could move in to cut off its escape route. Once the prey had been singled out, it rarely stood a chance.

Allosaurus could run at top speed only over short distances. A lengthy pursuit would not have been possible because of the dinosaur's huge bulk. Instead it relied on a rapid charge, ready to disable the panicked prey with one terrifying strike. When its victim was within reach, *Allosaurus* would fall upon the prey, grasping it with its forearms as it tore off chunks of flesh with its monstrous mouth. The huge, razor-sharp teeth could cut through flesh like a knife.

The jaws of *Allosaurus* were designed to pull back with the top set of teeth, while gripping the flesh of the victim with the lower set. In this way the dinosaur could saw and slice through flesh while holding the struggling prey fast. The head of the meat-eater was packed with muscles, to withstand the impact of the massive, jaw-wrenching attack it delivered.

Dinosaur Facts

Allosaurus may have hunted in packs. The bones of a number of Allosaurus have been found together, suggesting that the meat-eaters lived in a group.

The first fossil remains of Allosaurus were found in 1877 in Colorado, USA.

Fossil skeletons of Allosaurus have now been found in East Africa and even in south-east Australia.

The Australian Allosaurus remains suggest a smaller version of this meat-eater, perhaps less than one ton in weight.

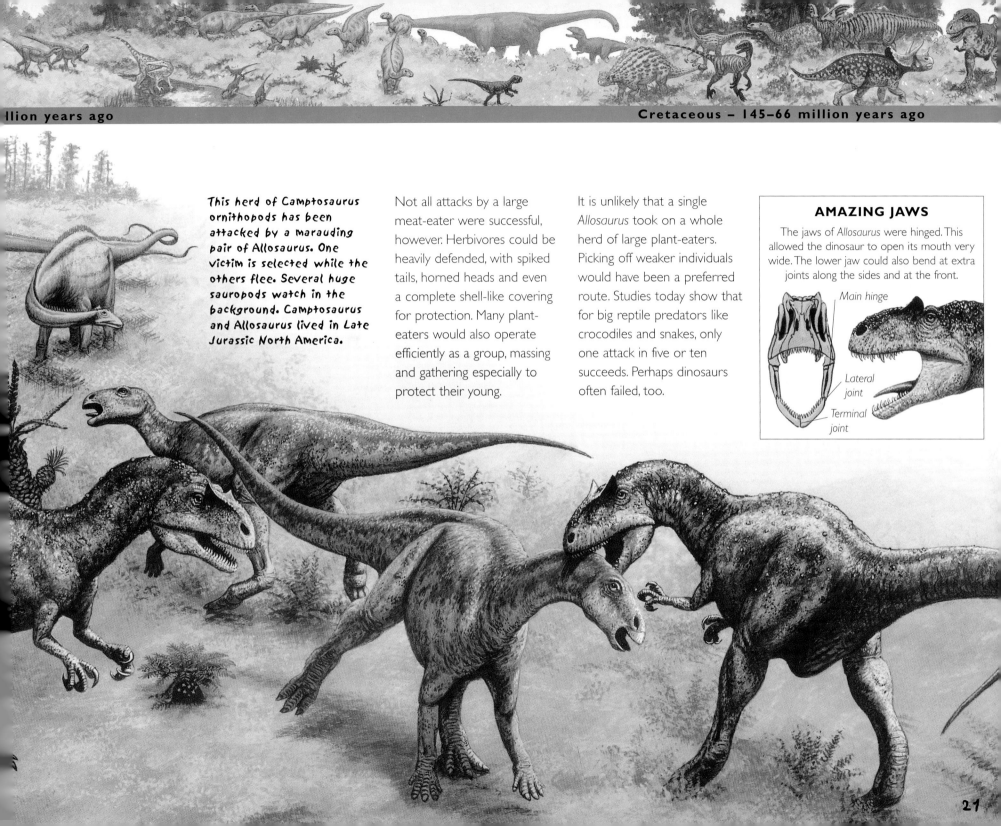

This herd of Camptosaurus ornithopods has been attacked by a marauding pair of Allosaurus. One victim is selected while the others flee. Several huge sauropods watch in the background. Camptosaurus and Allosaurus lived in Late Jurassic North America.

Not all attacks by a large meat-eater were successful, however. Herbivores could be heavily defended, with spiked tails, horned heads and even a complete shell-like covering for protection. Many plant-eaters would also operate efficiently as a group, massing and gathering especially to protect their young.

It is unlikely that a single *Allosaurus* took on a whole herd of large plant-eaters. Picking off weaker individuals would have been a preferred route. Studies today show that for big reptile predators like crocodiles and snakes, only one attack in five or ten succeeds. Perhaps dinosaurs often failed, too.

AMAZING JAWS

The jaws of *Allosaurus* were hinged. This allowed the dinosaur to open its mouth very wide. The lower jaw could also bend at extra joints along the sides and at the front.

Main hinge

Lateral joint

Terminal joint

21

Pack Hunters

Streamlined and agile, light-boned but powerful, Velociraptor was a lethal pack-hunter. Armed with its powerful sickle claw on each second toe, and a mouthful of smallish but sharp teeth, it was perhaps the wolf of its day.

their victims. The huge, curved claw on the second toe was used to rip into the flesh of its prey and tear it to bits. Sickle-clawed dinosaurs like Deinonychus also had relatively large brains, well developed for sight and hearing, and big eyes to hunt largely by vision. Perhaps their ability to think quickly, communicate as a group and work together as co-operative killers, all ensured their success as hunters.

A long, bony, fairly stiff tail helped the raptor to balance, and also to turn in a flash through a wide angle when running. As the tail swung to one side it would twist the body to the other side, like a counterweight. It would also work like the rudder of a plane to change the direction of motion. The light, long-legged build enabled the raptor to sprint, weave and duck, to avoid blows as the prey fought back.

Dinosaur Facts

A Deinonychus pack could have ripped a human being to pieces in 30 seconds!

Like modern stealthy predators, dinosaurs such as Deinonychus and Velociraptor may have been camouflaged to disguise themselves as they followed prey.

In one fossil find of Velociraptor, the dinosaur seems to have been found engaged in battle with a small horned dinosaur, known as Protoceratops.

The two dinosaurs appear to have been killed by a sandstorm, perhaps as the Protoceratops fought to protect its eggs.

Of all meat-eating dinosaurs, the terrible 'sickle-clawed' dromaeosaurs or raptors, such as Velociraptor and Deinonychus, seem to have been the most organized (see previous page). The group are named after

Dromaeosaurus, one of the first of their kind to be found and identified as a fossil. Individually, these terrifying creatures would eat any lizard or mammal that crossed their path. But they are better known for their combined force as a lethal hunting pack.

This is suggested by fossil sites which contain the remains of several raptors, as a group, rather than just single, isolated individuals. The lithe, streamlined bodies of the dromaeosaurs allowed them to race across the ground and leap through the air towards

Many
smallish
teeth

Belly ribs
(gastralia)

Stiffened joints
between tail bones

Powerful
arms

Long shin suggests fast running

Large
hands

Second toe 'sickle' claw

Three long-
clawed fingers

Deinonychus had a light, slender skeleton
with long arms and legs. Designed for
speed and agility, this dinosaur could leap well and run fast.
It lived about 110 million years ago, during the Early
Cretaceous, in North America. Its total length was 3m (10ft)
and it weighed an estimated 60-70kg (130-150lb).

Raptors had rows of sharp,
slicing teeth, but these were
not their main killing tools.
Their knife-sharp, razor-edged
claw on the second toe was
one of the most lethal
weapons of the prehistoric
age. The raptor may have used
its front claws to grip the prey
and hold tight, while slicing
into the flesh with kicks of the
back legs that brought the
knife-like claws into action,
slashing open the belly.

Despite
a relatively
small size,
Velociraptor was
probably able to kill much
larger prey. Its large nostrils
show that smell, as well as sight,
played a part in finding food. Like the
hyena today, this raptor may have
scavenged as well as actively hunted.

Small Carnivores

Dinosaur Facts

Coelophysis had surprisingly light, hollow bones and weighed only 25kg (55lb).

Coelophysis had four fingers on each hand. Only three were strong enough to grasp prey.

The first Oviraptor skeleton was found in the Gobi Desert in 1923.

The remains of Herrerasaurus were found by Victorino Herrera in Argentina.

Herrerasaurus had a sliding lower jaw that could bite prey, then move against the upper jaw to saw up a victim.

Not all of the meat-eating dinosaurs were huge giants like *Giganotosaurus*, *Tyrannosaurus* and *Allosaurus*. Nor were they medium-sized predators such as *Deinonychus* and the other raptors. There were dozens of kinds of smaller, less-known carnivorous dinosaurs which thrived during the Mesozoic era. One of the earliest was *Eoraptor*, 'dawn thief', which was no larger than a goose! It was extremely light with small, hollow bones, built for agility and speed. Like almost all carnivorous dinosaurs,

Eoraptor walked upright on its hind legs and used its front limbs as arms to search for, grasp and hold its prey.

Another very early carnivore was *Herrerasaurus*, which lived about 230 million years ago in South America – the same time and place as *Eoraptor*. It too was armed with sharp teeth, had short arms and stood on its two hind legs. At about 3.5m (11ft) long and 1.2m (4ft) tall, *Herrerasaurus* was as long and high as a small sports car, although much thinner. It probably weighed around 90–100kg 200–220lb). A skilled hunter, it tracked

down or ambushed prey like the four-legged, sheep-sized herbivores known as the rhynchosaurs. These were also reptiles, but not members of the dinosaur group. Several other dinosaurs from the Middle Triassic period have been found in South America.

Coelophysis was a small meat-eater that also grew up to 3m (10ft) in length. But it was much slimmer and lighter than

Herrerasaurus, and it lived in North America a few million years later. Like many of the small carnivores, it was built for speed and agility. A huge number of *Coelophysis* skeletons have been found in groups which include young dinosaurs as well as adults, suggesting that this particular meat-eater lived and hunted in packs. *Coelophysis* probably ate any small, snack-sized prey.

SIZE COMPARISON

One of the smallest dinosaurs of all was *Compsognathus* – it was not much bigger than a chicken! Like most other meat-eaters, it walked upright on its two hind legs, using its smaller arms to scrabble and grip.

Eoraptor

Herrerasaurus

Also among the small hunters is a group called oviraptors, a name meaning 'egg thieves'. *Oviraptor* itself was a strange-looking creature, with a large crest on its forehead. It also had a sharp, bony beak, in place of the rows of teeth normally seen in meat-eating dinosaurs. The first oviraptor skeleton found was discovered near a stash of eggs. Some dinosaur experts believed it had been about to steal the eggs for food. Newer evidence shows that the eggs were probably those of *Oviraptor* itself, and it was guarding its own nest. Its fossil skeleton had a smashed skull, perhaps the result of an attack from a predator. Even so, it is quite possible that this lithe carnivore stole the eggs of other dinosaurs for food (see page 47), so 'egg thief' is still an apt name.

Oviraptor guarding eggs

Coelophysis

Coelophysis had a long, slim skull with many small but sharp teeth, and relatively large eyes. Its neck was also long and very flexible. It may have made rapid 'pecking' movements like a bird, to snap up prey.

One fossilized Oviraptor skeleton found in Mongolia showed this dinosaur sitting on a nest of eggs. It is believed that Oviraptor stole the eggs of other dinosaurs for food, but this scene shows it guarding its own eggs in the nest. It may have had feathers to keep both itself and its eggs warm during incubation.

25

Amazing Vegetarians

Dinosaur Facts

Brachiosaurus ate up to a ton of plant food daily.

Herds of sauropods may have eaten the vegetation of each feeding area until it was nearly bare. They would then migrate to new territory.

Triceratops had self-sharpening teeth! The softer side of the tooth wore down faster than the hard side, which always left a sharp edge for cutting.

Duck-billed dinosaurs had large chewing teeth at the back of their jaws. They ate many different kinds of plants, including pine needles, magnolia leaves, seeds and fruits.

When most people think of dinosaurs they imagine huge fierce meat-eaters like *Tyrannosaurus*. However, there were many gentler, more peaceful plant-eating dinosaurs which roamed the prehistoric planet, searching for food in the form of vegetation. Whereas the meat-eaters could quickly break down and digest the flesh from their prey, plant matter such as stems, twigs and leaves does not break down so easily in the gut. The plant-eaters dealt with this problem in a variety of ways.

Some, like the sauropods, did not chew their food, but simply swallowed it whole, and relied on swallowing small stones too, to grind up the food in the gizzard (muscular stomach).

Diplodocus

Brachiosaurus

Stegosaurus

Plateosaurus

Following the dry Triassic period, lush vegetation and a mild climate created perfect conditions for Jurassic plant-eaters like Brachiosaurus and Stegosaurus.

Lesothosaurus

Flowering plants appeared on Earth for the first time during the Cretaceous period. A variety of new dinosaurs, such as *Triceratops*, *Edmontosaurus* and *Euoplocephalus*, evolved to take advantage of this new food source.

Titanosaurus

Ouranosaurus

Euoplocephalus

Hypsilophodon

Protoceratops

Edmontosaurus

Stegoceras

Parasaurolophus

DIFFERENT TEETH

Prosauropod *Sauropod* *Hadrosaur*

The teeth of plant-eaters varied from species to species. Prosauropod teeth had serrated (jagged) edges for cutting into tough shoots and leaves. Sauropods had peg-like teeth for pulling and raking. Hadrosaurs had rows of cheek teeth that could chew tough vegetation such as bark, pine cones and conifer needles.

Other herbivores, like the hadrosaurs (duck-billed dinosaurs) such as *Edmontosaurus*, ground and chopped up their food in their mouths before swallowing it. They had rows of hundreds of teeth, called dental batteries.

There were many different groups of plant-eaters in the dinosaur world. The huge sauropods such as *Titanosaurus* and *Brachiosaurus* were giraffe-like and roamed in herds, constantly searching for food to maintain their great bulk.

They had smallish teeth shaped like pencils or pegs, which worked like a garden rake to strip leaves and fronds from their stems. The food would be swallowed whole and ground up by stomach stones in the gizzard.

One of the most famous of the plant-eaters is the amazing *Triceratops*, a ceratopsian (horned) dinosaur. Its fossils were first discovered in North

America in the 1880s. Like many other plant-eaters, *Triceratops* probably grazed in herds, through the lush forests that grew in North America towards the end of the dinosaur age. *Triceratops* used the sharp, toothless beak at the front of its mouth to cut through even the toughest vegetation. This was sliced, chopped and shredded with its many cheek teeth, worked by powerful jaw muscles.

Dinosaur teeth seem to have grown continuously. When old ones wore away and fell out, new teeth grew to take their place. So, like crocodiles and alligators today, the teeth in a dinosaur's mouth would be different sizes and ages. Some hadrosaurs had more than one thousand cheek teeth – far more than any large reptile alive today.

Triceratops

Gentle Giants

The sauropods were a group of plant-eating dinosaurs that had small heads, long necks and tails, four pillar-like legs and huge, bulky bodies. They were without doubt the largest and heaviest land animals ever to have lived, and the most successful of the plant-eating dinosaurs during the late Triassic and Jurassic periods.

Brachiosaurus was one of the tallest sauropods, with an immense height of 13m (43ft), as tall as a four-floor building! *Brachiosaurus* had four thick, sturdy legs which each supported more than 10 tons. Like a giraffe, it may have used its enormous neck to reach high into the trees for food, stripping vegetation from the branches as it moved its head from side to side. *Diplodocus* was much slimmer, but longer, at 27m (88ft).

It is famous for its whiplash tail, which it used to balance its body

If a Brachiosaurus were alive today it could lift its head high enough to look over a four-floor building. However, a few other sauropods, including Mamenchisaurus and Sauroposeidon, were even taller!

Plateosaurus, a Triassic prosauropod

Dinosaur Facts

The tail alone of Diplodocus contained up to 80 vertebrae (backbones). The similar sauropod Apatosaurus had even more – 82 vertebrae.

Apatosaurus was once called 'Brontosaurus', meaning 'thunder lizard'.

Anchisaurus was a prosauropod that walked on all fours, even though its front legs were much smaller than its hind legs. Its name means 'near lizard'.

The brain of a sauropod such as Brachiosaurus was minute compared to the overall size of the dinosaur – only 1/100,000th the weight of the entire body!

and also to defend itself against attacking meat-eaters. It had a long snake-like neck to match its endless tail and, like all sauropods, walked on four thick-set, elephant-like legs.

If you look at a cantilever bridge, you can see how the head, neck, body and tail of *Diplodocus* were 'designed'. Four supporting legs held up the body or 'bridge', with the body supported by a row of large, strong vertebrae

(backbones). Despite its huge length, *Diplodocus* weighed only as much as three or four elephants – perhaps 10–15 tons. Like other sauropods, it had a tiny brain and its reactions must have been very slow.

Sauropods were descended from a group of smaller plant-eaters called prosauropods. These earlier creatures lived mainly during the Late Triassic and Early Jurassic periods. An example is *Anchisaurus*, one of

the smallest and most primitive of the group, from about 200–188 million years ago. The North American landscape where *Anchisaurus* lived was also occupied by hunting meat-eaters, which would almost certainly have fed on this plant-eater. Without the larger body mass of the later sauropods, *Anchisaurus* would either run away in the event of an attack, or stand in a defensive posture with its sickle claws held out to ward off the predator.

Other prosauropods include *Plateosaurus*, about 8m (26ft) long, which lived 214–204 million years ago in Europe, and similar dinosaurs from even earlier, in Madagascar.

BRACHIOSAURUS

Peg-like teeth at front of mouth

DIPLODOCUS

Nasal opening

Eye socket (orbit)

No chewing cheek teeth

Diplodocus and Brachiosaurus both used their long, thin teeth like a rake, to pull vast quantities of vegetation into the mouth. Both had nostrils high on the head. This may have helped them to breathe more easily while feeding among leaves.

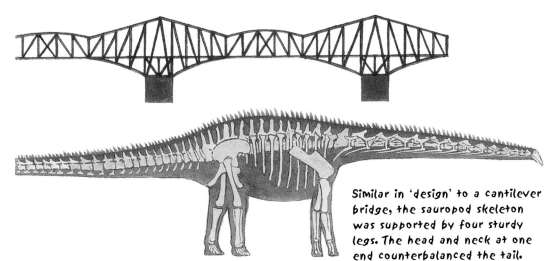

Similar in 'design' to a cantilever bridge, the sauropod skeleton was supported by four sturdy legs. The head and neck at one end counterbalanced the tail.

DINOSAUR SCALE

Diplodocus is one of the longest sauropods known from fairly complete fossil remains. It measured up to 27m (88ft) in total length. *Brachiosaurus* was one of the tallest, standing almost 13m (43ft) high when stretching into the tree tops. Both of these dinosaurs would dwarf the largest land animal alive today, the elephant. Some sauropods, known from partial remains, were even bigger!

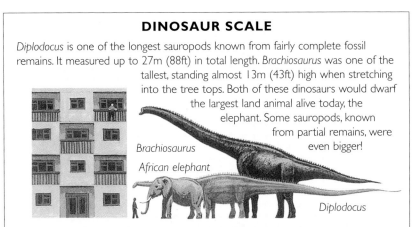

Brachiosaurus

African elephant

Diplodocus

Living Together

The dinosaur landscape was filled with large herds of roaming plant-eaters. They were shadowed by predatory meat-eaters such as Albertosaurus, waiting for a chance to pounce.

Exactly how the dinosaurs lived together is a mystery. Unless we could observe dinosaurs in the flesh, as we do with modern animals, it is virtually impossible to know how they may have behaved, both within a group and among different species. However, modern animals can help us to imagine how dinosaurs might have lived.

Dinosaur Facts

Tracks left by herds of plant-eaters show larger footprints on the outside, and smaller footprints in the middle. This suggests that plant-eating herds moved as a group, with young dinosaurs protected in the middle.

Dinosaur males may have fought among themselves over females and territory, much like the males of many modern animals do.

Some plant-eating dinosaurs like the hadrosaurs (duck-bills) migrated huge distances as a herd, to return to nesting colonies where they laid their eggs.

Centrosaurus

Corythosaurus

Euoplocephalus

Albertosaurus

Mamm

The plains of Africa are a good place to start, where many different kinds of animal live together in a delicate co-existence. Just like the dinosaur world, modern wild animals are made up of plant-eaters, which often live in groups, and meat-eaters, which can survive as part of a group, but also alone.

The discovery of thousands of fossil bones, representing the mass graves of plant-eating dinosaurs, show that certain species lived together in herds. Perhaps they worked as a group to protect themselves and their young. As with modern animals, we can picture how different dinosaur species relied upon each other for survival – and especially how fierce hunters picked off members of a plant-eating group. This way of life may seem to be a cruel and one-sided existence for the herbivores, yet their very presence and survival depend on the carnivores. If a plant-eating herd grew too large, there simply would not be enough food for them, and they would slowly die of starvation. Also, by weeding out the weak and sick, the hunters kept the rest of the herd fit and healthy. We can imagine that much the same balance occurred with the dinosaurs. Co-dependence (depending upon each other for survival) relied upon a balance of prey and predators.

Herds of duck-billed plant-eaters like *Parasaurolophus* and *Corythosaurus* functioned as a group, with each dinosaur co-operating to look out for meat-eaters and search for food. These duck-bills had hollow crests of bone on the head. Different shapes and sizes of crests may have been used to show the group whether the dinosaur was male or female, as in modern-day antelopes. It is also possible that the crest could produce sound, allowing the dinosaurs to communicate with their own kind, and perhaps warn each other about approaching predators and other dangers.

Pteranodon

Corythosaurus

Stegoceras

Crocodile

Turtle

Prehistoric Protection

With a range of hungry, determined predators on the loose, many plant-eating dinosaurs developed amazing ways to protect themselves from attack. Some plant-eaters were covered from head to tail in armour; others were protected by bony shields and plates around their necks and heads, and still others were armed with sharp horns and spikes, which could deliver a fatal wound. The armoured dinosaurs fell into three main groups

– the scelidosaurs, stegosaurs and ankylosaurs. *Scelidosaurus* belonged to the scelidosaur group. About 4m (13ft) long, it was covered with rows of tough, sharp bones which grew from its skin. It had a small, narrow head and beak-like mouth and probably fed on soft plants and fruits.

Under attack, *Scelidosaurus* would have crouched on the ground, presenting only its thick, tough, scaly skin to any

meat-eater. With sharp spikes tough enough to break the attacker's teeth, it would not have made easy prey.

Ankylosaurs were the most heavily defended dinosaurs, with thick bony plates that covered the neck, back, sides, and tails. These dinosaurs had extremely thick skin, into which the flat plates of bone were set. Spikes and sharp knobs also stuck out, to warn

any hungry meat-eater that the plant-eater would be a difficult target. All this protection made the ankylosaurs very heavy. Their weights ranged from 2 tons to more than 5 tons in larger types like *Edmontonia*.

Some ankylosaurs had an extra weapon at the end of the tail – a thick, heavy, hammer-like club of bone. A single blow from this heavy tail club could be enough to fell a large meat-eater.

Sauropelta

Scelidosaurus

Polacanthus

Stegosaurus

Huayangosaurus

Kentrosaurus

Ankylosaurus

perhaps even crippling it for good. Most ankylosaurs lived during the Cretaceous period, towards the end of the age

of the dinosaurs. Their fossils have been found in North America, Asia and Australia.

Kentrosaurus belonged to the stegosaur group. It had very long, dagger-like spikes that grew from the middle of its back to the tip of its tail. In front of these bony daggers were diamond-shaped plates that were similar to those of a *Stegosaurus*. If approached from behind, this formidable

plant-eater could have backed into its attacker, piercing it with its long, sharp spikes and swinging its spiny tail.

Many plant-eating dinosaurs were protected from attacking meat-eaters by their tough body armour. Some had sharp, bony spikes along the back and sides, while others were covered in a mass of bony plates. The heavy tail club was unique to ankylosaurs.

Thorny Issues

The name Stegosaurus means 'roof lizard'. The huge triangular plates were once thought to lie flat on the back, like the tiles on a roof.

Stegosaurus plates formed two rows, which ran from the neck, along either side of the back, to the tail.

It has recently been discovered that Stegosaurus had a pattern of disc-shaped bones to protect its hips, and disc-shaped studs around its neck.

There are several ideas about why Stegosaurus had back plates – but no general agreement among the experts.

Some of the most spectacular dinosaurs were the stegosaurs. These amazing creatures had a row of tall, bony spikes or plates, that ran from the top of the neck, along the back and down to the end of the tail. Stegosaurs lived during the Middle Jurassic and Early Cretaceous periods, about 176 to 100 million years ago. Their fossils have been found across most of the world, but especially in North America and east Asia.

Stegosaurs had large, weighty bodies and huge hind legs that were nearly twice as long as the front legs. At the very tip of a stegosaur's tail were a number of long, sharp spikes, which the dinosaur probably used to protect itself against meat-eaters. All stegosaurs were plant-eaters, munching on low, soft vegetation.

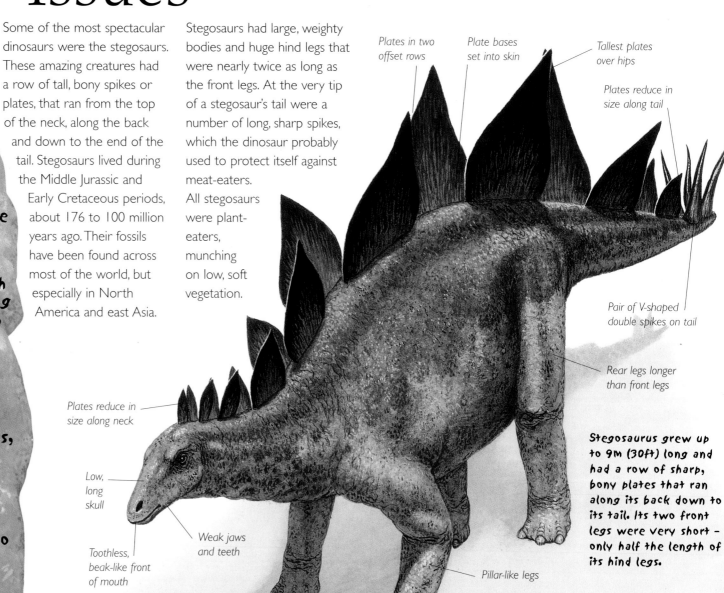

Plates in two offset rows

Plate bases set into skin

Tallest plates over hips

Plates reduce in size along tail

Pair of V-shaped double spikes on tail

Rear legs longer than front legs

Plates reduce in size along neck

Low, long skull

Weak jaws and teeth

Toothless, beak-like front of mouth

Pillar-like legs

Stegosaurus grew up to 9m (30ft) long and had a row of sharp, bony plates that ran along its back down to its tail. Its two front legs were very short – only half the length of its hind legs.

34

Stegosaurus is the best-known dinosaur of the stegosaur family. Among its many surprising features was its tiny brain, hardly larger than a human thumb! Compared to the huge size and bulk of *Stegosaurus*, this was one of the smallest brains of any dinosaur.

Over the years, dinosaur experts have argued over the true function of the back plates of *Stegosaurus*. Many theories about their use have been put forward. Some people think the plates were body armour, used to protect the dinosaur during attack. However, the bone forming the core of the plate is quite light and spongy, and not especially strong. Also the position of the plates, jutting straight up from the back, is not very protective.

The plates might have been used to control body temperature. They could soak up the heat of the sun to warm up the dinosaur if it was cool, or let out the heat if *Stegosaurus* became too hot and stood in the shade.

Another suggestion is that *Stegosaurus* used its plates to 'scare off' enemies or rival males. The plates might even change coloration, like the skin of various reptiles today. It has even been considered that the plates helped *Stegosaurus* rise on to its hind legs, to feed from vegetation.

Like all stegosaurs, Tuojiangosaurus had a four-pronged tail which it used to defend itself against meat-eaters such as Yangchuanosaurus. Tuojiangosaurus was the first stegosaur to be discovered in Asia – its fossils come from China. It was some 7m (23ft) long and lived about 160 million years ago, near the end of the Jurassic period.

THE SIZE OF STEGOSAURUS

Stegosaurus was the largest of the stegosaurs, or plated dinosaurs. It was about 9m (30ft) in total length and weighed around 2 tons. It was tallest at the hips, where the 1m (3ft) long plates added to the size of the back legs, to give a total height of some 4m (13ft).

Yangchuanosaurus

Tuojiangosaurus

Horns and Frills

The great horned dinosaurs like *Centrosaurus*, *Triceratops* and *Protoceratops* are some of the most inspiring and well-known plant-eaters of the dinosaur age. These creatures, also called ceratopsians, are easily recognized by the features of the head – a beaked mouth, a range of horns on the face, and a large, bony frill behind the neck. All were plant-eaters and walked on four sturdy legs. Many lived in groups.

Triceratops is the largest and perhaps best-known of the horned dinosaurs. As heavy as an elephant, and with a huge head that grew as long as an adult human being, *Triceratops* lived in herds towards the very end of the dinosaur age. It probably spent much of its time searching for vegetation in the forests that flourished in the later, cooler Cretaceous period, eating even the toughest plants, which it sliced up with its beak-like snout. *Triceratops* had three horns, one on the snout and two above its eyes, giving the name which means 'three horned face'.

Triceratops almost certainly used its body armour to defend itself against predatory meat-eaters, but may also have used these features to warn off rival males if threatened. *Triceratops* certainly had a much larger brain than the less developed stegosaurs.

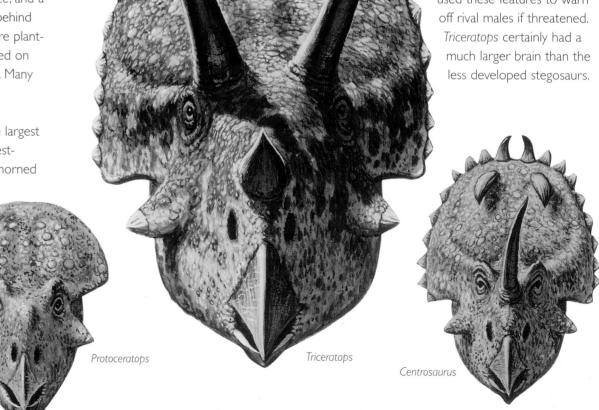

Protoceratops

Triceratops

Centrosaurus

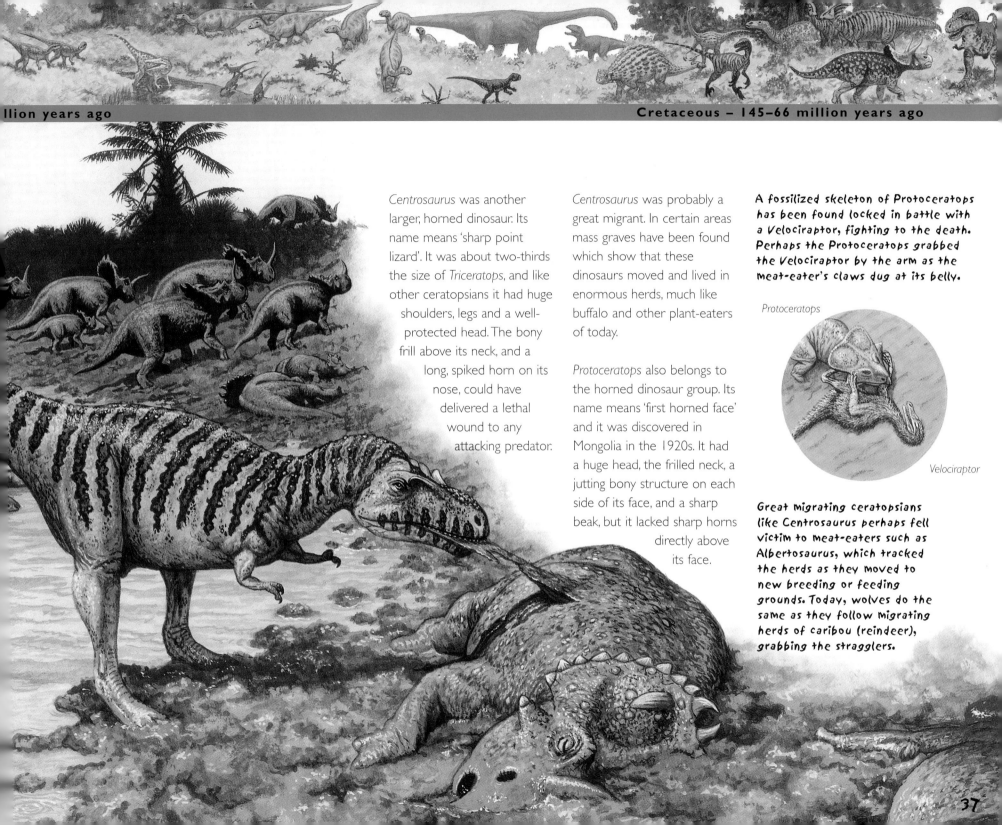

Centrosaurus was another larger, horned dinosaur. Its name means 'sharp point lizard'. It was about two-thirds the size of *Triceratops*, and like other ceratopsians it had huge shoulders, legs and a well-protected head. The bony frill above its neck, and a long, spiked horn on its nose, could have delivered a lethal wound to any attacking predator.

Centrosaurus was probably a great migrant. In certain areas mass graves have been found which show that these dinosaurs moved and lived in enormous herds, much like buffalo and other plant-eaters of today.

Protoceratops also belongs to the horned dinosaur group. Its name means 'first horned face' and it was discovered in Mongolia in the 1920s. It had a huge head, the frilled neck, a jutting bony structure on each side of its face, and a sharp beak, but it lacked sharp horns directly above its face.

A fossilized skeleton of Protoceratops has been found locked in battle with a Velociraptor, fighting to the death. Perhaps the Protoceratops grabbed the Velociraptor by the arm as the meat-eater's claws dug at its belly.

Protoceratops

Velociraptor

Great migrating ceratopsians like Centrosaurus perhaps fell victim to meat-eaters such as Albertosaurus, which tracked the herds as they moved to new breeding or feeding grounds. Today, wolves do the same as they follow migrating herds of caribou (reindeer), grabbing the stragglers.

37

Fight to the Death

Although the meat-eating dinosaurs have a reputation as unstoppable hunters, some of their victims were able to put up an impressive fight against their attackers. The horned dinosaurs (ceratopsians) such as *Triceratops* and its relatives used their formidable weapons to slash and stab at any meat-eater presenting a threat. Other dinosaurs, like *Euoplocephalus* and *Ankylosaurus*, were heavily protected, covered almost from head to toe in a huge weight of bony structures that were virtually impossible to bite through or break. In fact, armoured dinosaurs like *Euoplocephalus* had two lines of protection against the great meat-eaters such as *Tyrannosaurus*. The first

was to lie close to the ground, thereby protecting the only soft part of the body – the belly. Every other part of *Euoplocephalus* was covered in strong armour. The main hope for the meat-eater would be to turn an unfortunate *Euoplocephalus* on to its back, then sink its claws and teeth into the soft flesh of its underside. But *Euoplocephalus* weighed more than 2 tons, and it could squat down and dig in, to anchor itself into the ground with its strong limbs.

Triceratops could maim or kill a predator by defending itself with its sharp facial horns.

Triceratops possibly protected their young from attacking meat-eaters by forming a protective circle. They shielded the young from attack with their sharp horns.

Attacker

Young in middle

Adults facing outwards

Male Triceratops might have fought each other to win the females of the herd. They could battle by locking their horns together, shoving and pushing, much like rams today.

Dinosaur Facts

The various pieces of body protection of Euoplocephalus were linked together like a mosaic, allowing it to be flexible while still forming a protective shield.

Some dinosaurs, such as Minmi, had bony plates that even covered and protected the animal's underside.

Wounds delivered by an armoured dinosaur could cause huge damage to a meat-eater. One Tyrannosaurus skeleton has been found with a wound to its back so severe that its head and neck were forced up and backwards.

Euoplocephalus had a second line of defence – attack! At the base of its bony tail was an enormous club, made up of two heavy bones fused together. The tail was more than 2.5m (8ft) long, and powerful enough to lash out with great force. This is known from its fossil bones, which have large flat projections to anchor their muscles.

Just one blow from the tail of *Euoplocephalus* would be enough to disable a large meat-eater, smashing the bones within its body and bringing it crashing to the ground. Several ankylosaurs had such tail clubs. Members of the ankylosaur group that lacked the tail club, and lived during earlier times, are known as nodosaurs.

Other large, armoured plant-eaters like *Triceratops* and *Centrosaurus* were also built to survive attack. *Triceratops* in particular would have protected itself by standing face-on to any attacker, presenting its huge bony neck shield and bony horns as both threat and protection. Many *Triceratops* probably worked as a group to defend themselves,

HAMMER-TAIL

The tail bones of *Euoplocephalus* weighed up to 30kg (65lb) – half as much as an adult human. They formed an enormous club, composed mainly of two bones that were fused or sealed together, to form a large bulge at the end. *Euoplocephalus* almost certainly used this club against aggressive meat-eaters. The tail could swing from side to side at the base, but the end was stiffer.

standing in a circle to face outwards at a threat. Faced with such opposition, even a large predator would have been reluctant to take its chances. We can see a similar strategy today on the frozen Arctic tundra, where musk oxen stand in a circle, facing outwards with horns ready, to protect themselves against wolves or polar bears.

The tail hammer of Euoplocephalus was powerful enough to shatter the bones of any predator that came too close. By lashing its tail from side to side, it could easily bring down a large meat-eater such as Tyrannosaurus, cracking its shin or thigh.

Not all plant-eaters depended on body armour for protection from the meat-eaters. Smaller or medium-sized dinosaurs like Dryosaurus would have used the tried and tested method of running away if any predator come too close! This herbivore, about 4m (13ft) long, lived in North America and Africa during the Jurassic period. It may have been a cousin of Iguanodon.

Bone-headed Dinosaurs

The bone-headed dinosaurs were a group of strange-looking creatures, whose heads were crowned with a shield of tough, thick bone – rather like a helmet. These dinosaurs probably walked semi-upright on two legs. The group includes the homalocephalids and the pachycephalosaurs, which had even larger bony heads than their homalocephalid relatives.

Dinosaur experts are still unsure why these dinosaurs needed such large, tough heads. Some think they may have been used to defend against meat-eaters. But it seems unlikely that the bony helmet would have been any use against a hungry predator. The bone-headed dinosaur would have probably run away, rather than head-butt its ferocious attacker!

It is possible that the bony heads were used to knock vegetation, such as fruits and seeds, from trees. Then the dinosaur could feed on the fallen items.

Dinosaur Facts

There are about ten known kinds of bone-headed dinosaurs. All lived in the Late Cretaceous period.

Bone-headed dinosaur skeletons have been found in Europe, North America and East Asia.

The largest bone-headed dinosaur, Pachycephalosaurus, had a skull roof or covering that was 25cm (10in) thick.

Some bone-headed dinosaurs, like Stygimoloch and Homalocephale, had spiked ridges that grew at the back and sides of the head.

The skull cap of Stegoceras grew thicker and higher with age.

Pachycephalosaurus and the homalocephalids probably lived on vegetation, although we cannot be certain exactly what they ate. With small, ridged teeth, these dinosaurs could not eat the tough, fibrous plant matter that the duck-billed and horned dinosaurs tackled. It is more likely that the bone-heads fed on a mixture of shoots, leaves, seeds and perhaps even small animals such as insects. The largest of the bone-heads was *Pachycephalosaurus*, at 4.5m (15ft) long.

Another suggestion for the bony head cap is that males competed for females during the mating season by bashing their heads together, like modern-day rams (male sheep). The skull of the bone-headed dinosaur was joined to its neck with tough, strong ligaments, which could absorb sudden pressure in the event of a collision. With this extraordinary built-in stock absorber, the male could have used his spectacular crown to dominate rivals.

The part of the brain that can detect smell was particularly large in these dinosaurs, which probably helped them to pick up the scent of a distant meat-eater. One of the best-known bone-heads is *Stegoceras* which was about 2.4m (8ft) long. It lived in what are now the states of Montana and Alberta, in North America. Its fossils were named in 1902.

BONE-HEAD HEADS

The curious skulls of the bone-headed dinosaurs came in many shapes and sizes. *Pachycephalosaurus* had a very large skull that could grow up to 60cm (24in) long! The skulls of its relatives were smaller. *Homalocephale* and *Stegoceras* had skulls that were very thick and covered in bony pits and knobs. *Prenocephale* had a row of strange ridges that ran from above its eyes to the back of its head.

Pachycephalosaurus

Homalocephale   Stegoceras   Prenocephale

Bone-headed dinosaurs may have rammed trees, to bring down the fruits on which they fed (opposite). In addition, or alternatively, they may have had head-butting contests at breeding time (left).

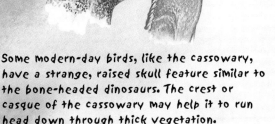

Some modern-day birds, like the cassowary, have a strange, raised skull feature similar to the bone-headed dinosaurs. The crest or casque of the cassowary may help it to run head down through thick vegetation.

41

Duck-billed Dinosaurs

The duck-billed dinosaurs belong to a group also known as the hadrosaurs. These creatures could grow up to 15m (50ft) long, and they were all plant-eaters. They were equipped with wide, toothless beaks and a large number of flat cheek teeth which they used to grind up very tough vegetation With its large, curved, upright bony

crest *Corythosaurus* was an easily recognized duck-bill. Individuals could have different crest shapes and sizes, probably depending on the age and sex of each one. (It was once thought that there were seven or more species of this dinosaur because so many different crest shapes were found among its skeletons!)

The crest may have been used to identify each dinosaur in the herd, helping other herd members to work out how old an individual was, and whether it was female or male. The males of the herd had especially large crests, which they may have used to communicate. By blowing air from the windpipe through the hollow crest and then out through the nose, a loud trumpet-like

noise could result – a sound that might have been used for warning of danger.

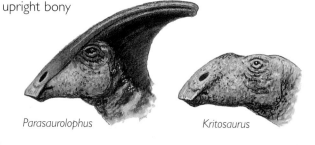

Parasaurolophus

Kritosaurus

Maiasaura

Saurolophus

Duck-billed dinosaurs are best known for their amazing head crests. Parasaurolophus was one of the largest, and easily recognized by its long, tube-like crest. Not all duck-bills had a head crest, however. Maiasaura and Kritosaurus lacked this body part.

The crest of Corythosaurus was shaped like half a dinner plate stuck into the top of its head!

Dinosaur Facts

After hatching, Maiasaura babies probably stayed in their nests for some weeks before venturing outside.

Lambeosaurus had a hollow, hatchet-shaped crest on top of its head, which it may have used as a sound-box to produce deep, horn-like noises.

The duck-billed dinosaur Kritosaurus had no crest on its head. But it did have a ridge-like bump on its nose, in front of its eyes. This may have been the anchor point for a bag or sac of skin, which the dinosaur inflated like a balloon to make a honking sound.

Hadrosaurs are best-known for their head crests, but some types lacked this feature. These are known as the hadrosaurids. They include *Maiasaura*, whose name means 'good mother lizard'. This gentle plant-eater probably roamed in herds along the coastal plains of the time, following the pastures of food that grew with the seasons. It may have migrated huge distances to return to the same nesting site year after year, to lay its eggs and bring up the babies.

Most hadrosaurs could walk on four legs or two, and stride along at a very good speed.

They were sizeable dinosaurs which were not easy prey. For example, *Lambeosaurus* was 15m (50ft) long and perhaps weighed more than 5 tons. It probably relied on safety-in-numbers to protect itself from roaming meat-eaters of the time, like *Tyrannosaurus*. The crest of *Lambeosaurus* had a triangular or hatchet-shaped front part, just in front of the eyes, with a bony lump or spur behind. Fossils of this duck-bill date from about 75 million years ago. They have been found at several sites in North America, as far south as Mexico.

A herd of Lambeosaurus treks across the plains of what is now the USA's Mid-West. The adult male's head crest has a tall, angular front part. The crests of the females are more rounded.

43

Dinosaur Babies

All dinosaurs probably laid eggs, as crocodiles do today, rather than giving birth to live young. So many fossilized dinosaur eggs have been found that dinosaur experts now believe this was the way in which the great reptiles reproduced. Some eggs still contain the skeleton of a baby dinosaur. It can be seen inside the shell, by modern techniques such as high-powered medical scanners. Dinosaur eggs seem surprisingly small when compared to the size of the adults. For example, a baby duck-bill dinosaur just hatched from its egg would only have been 35cm (14in) long. But if the eggs had been any bigger, the thick shells needed to support their weight would have prevented oxygen from reaching the baby inside.

At some fossil sites, the remains of hundreds of preserved nests, with

Duck-billed dinosaurs such as Maiasaura may have protected their babies from marauding predators like Albertosaurus.

eggs, have been discovered. They were spaced far enough apart to allow each dinosaur parent – probably the mother – to lie next to her nest without disturbing her nearby fellows.

Huge dinosaurs like the duck-bills could never have sat on their nests, like birds such as ducks and chickens today. They would have crushed the tiny eggs beneath them! It is not known if dinosaur parents stayed near their eggs for a lengthy time, to protect them – or even to keep them warm. We know that some crocodiles and alligators bury their eggs in warm sand or a nest mound of rotting vegetation, so perhaps dinosaurs did the same.

Breeding in large colonies, like sea birds such as gulls, has advantages. The large numbers of parents stand a better chance against scavenging meat-eaters, than one parent on its own. Also there are so many youngsters at hatching time that the predators cannot possibly attack and eat them all. Some are bound to survive.

Fossilized dinosaur nests and eggs can tell us a lot about the reproduction and rearing of young. But courtship and mating are much more of a mystery. We can really only compare dinosaurs with modern-day animals. It is likely that large hunters such as *Tyrannosaurus* would have a dangerous courtship, with the smaller male literally risking life and limb to 'court' a much larger female for the right to mate.

DINOSAUR EGGS
When placed next to the egg of a chicken, a dinosaur egg seems huge. But compared to the massively bulky adult dinosaur, the egg is relatively small. Its shell had to be strong, but thin enough to allow oxygen to seep in and reach the developing baby inside. If the egg had been any larger, the dinosaur baby would have suffocated.

Finding a mate could be a dangerous business for male meat-eating dinosaurs. Fossils show that the females of certain species, like Tyrannosaurus, were often much larger than the males. A male perhaps courted the female for many days, to persuade her to mate – and even then, she could turn on him at any moment.

Family Life

Dinosaur experts are still not sure how, or even if, some dinosaurs cared for their young. Most is known about gentle plant-eaters like *Maiasaura* and other duck-billed dinosaurs, through the discovery of large fossilized nesting colonies belonging to these creatures. When searching through remains found on 'Egg Mountain', USA, dinosaur expert

Like plant-eating dinosaurs, meat-eaters may also have nurtured their young, and even taught them to hunt and kill.

Dinosaur Facts

Maiasaura was a duck-billed dinosaur, or hadrosaur, that lived in North America about 76 million years ago during the Late Cretaceous period. It grew to about 9M (30ft) long.

Duck-billed dinosaurs probably identified their own babies among the colony by smell, or by distinguishing coloration or markings.

Maiasaura dinosaurs returned to lay their eggs and breed at the same site every season.

Oviraptor laid its eggs in a tight circle, propping them up with sand so that the baby inside could escape more easily when it broke out of the shell.

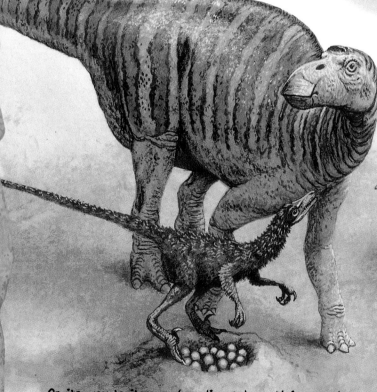

A Troodon parent prepares to defend its clutch of eggs against the passing Maiasaura.

John Horner found a number of eggs which he thought belonged to the plant-eater *Orodromeus*. But when an egg was opened or its interior scanned, the dinosaur baby inside showed that they were actually the eggs of *Troodon*, a small meat-eater. As dinosaur experts began to investigate further, they found that *Troodon* seemed to lay its eggs in a nest, just like the plant-eaters. It may have even nested in colonies with other *Troodon*.

Troodon may have had fluffy fur or feathers, to retain body heat, since it could have been warm-blooded.

On its way to its own breeding colony, Maiasaura has wandered into a nesting site of several Troodon. But the large herbivore presents no real threat.

46

If meat-eaters such as *Troodon* took such care to ensure the survival of their eggs and young, it is possible that other carnivores also tried to give their babies the best chance they could. We cannot be certain how larger meat-eaters like *Tyrannosaurus* and *Allosaurus* raised their young, if they did at all. But it is possible that a mother *Tyrannosaurus* would have guarded her nest of eggs until they hatched, as any dinosaur egg would have

been an easy source of food – not only for other dinosaurs, but for lizards, small mammals and other meat-eaters.

How the young were treated when they hatched is a mystery. Perhaps, like modern-day hunters, they would have learned to hunt by watching the mother, and feeding from her kills. Young *Tyrannosaurus* would certainly have been vulnerable to attack from

Oviraptor had a powerful curved beak which seemed very suitable for holding eggs. Two bony projections in the roof of the mouth would press down to crack or tear the shell, to release the nutritious contents.

other predators, so it is possible that their mother gave them some protection, just as crocodiles guard their babies today in a quiet 'nursery' pool.

Duck-billed dinosaurs reared their young among a herd, and protected them as they grew from hatchlings into juvenile dinosaurs. Colonies (groups) of duck-billed dinosaur nests have been found with the skeletons of baby dinosaurs inside. The parents of these

Just before hatching, a baby dinosaur would completely fill its egg shell. The head and tail curved around to fit into the limited space. The dwindling yellowish yolk in the middle still supplied food, for the last few days before hatching.

babies must have tended their young for a while, because the bones of the hatchlings are not well developed enough for them to run about, yet their teeth show wear marks from chewing foods.

Duck-billed dinosaurs such as Maiasaura reared their young in large herds. By working together as a group, the parents could remain alert to danger and warn each other if any meat-eater threatened.

NESTS, EGGS AND BABIES

Protoceratops nests have been found almost perfectly intact, fossilized with the eggs still positioned in a distinctive circular pattern. This dinosaur lived about 75–71 million years ago and its remains come from the Gobi Desert of Asia. Once hatched, a *Protoceratops* baby would have fitted into a human hand! Fossil finds reveal all stages of *Protoceratops* growth, from hatchlings to the 2m (6¹/₂ft) long adults.

Flying Lizards

Huge plant- and meat-eating dinosaurs may have ruled the land during the Mesozoic era. But the skies were the realm of enormous flying reptiles. They are known as pterosaurs, which means 'winged lizards'. But they were not lizards, nor were they dinosaurs. Pterosaurs were a distinct group of reptiles, and they were very successful. They first appeared with the early dinosaurs, in the Triassic period. This was some 70 million years before the first bird was ever seen. Pterosaurs ranged in size from no larger than a modern-day blackbird to enormous creatures with a wing span of 13m (43ft).

With their ability to glide and fly, the large pterosaurs could travel anywhere they wished. They would have been able to cover huge distances by simply soaring on air currents, helping themselves along with an occasional flap of their wings. They would also be able to feed as they flew, swooping down into the waters of oceans or lakes below, to scoop up fish and other prey using their enormous beaks.

Despite their huge heads, hefty beaks and muscular bodies, pterosaurs were surprisingly light. They were fully designed for life in the air. Their legs would allow them to walk on land and perhaps take a few running hops.

Dinosaur Facts

One of the first pterosaurs in the skies is known as Eudimorphodon. Some experts think it may have been around even before the dawn of the dinosaurs.

Large pterosaurs like Ornithocheirus may have been able to travel up to 500km (300 miles) each day, by gliding through the skies on their giant wings.

A fossilized parasite, similar to the ticks that feed on bats and birds today, has been found at the bottom of a lake in Russia. This blood-sucker probably fed on the pterosaurs.

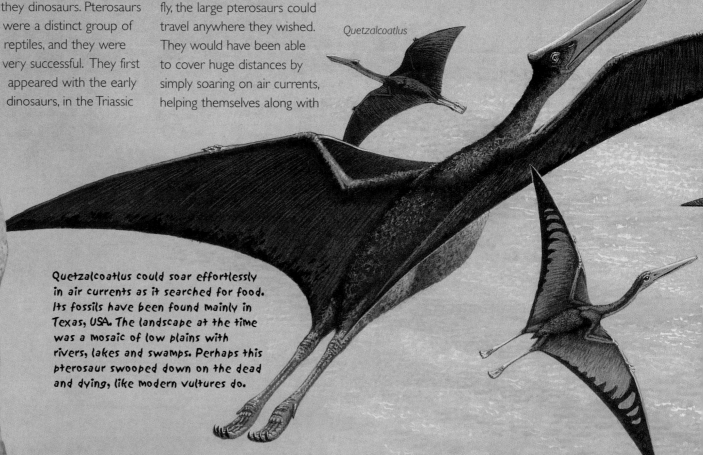

Quetzalcoatlus

Quetzalcoatlus could soar effortlessly in air currents as it searched for food. Its fossils have been found mainly in Texas, USA. The landscape at the time was a mosaic of low plains with rivers, lakes and swamps. Perhaps this pterosaur swooped down on the dead and dying, like modern vultures do.

Quetzalcoatlus, from 68–66 million years ago, takes the prize for the biggest wings in history. This amazing giant had a span of over 13m (43ft) when its wings were fully extended – which is longer than the span of many small aircraft today.

The pterosaurs fall into two main groups, rhamphorhynchs and pterodactyls. The rhamphorhynchs came first and were generally small, with short legs. The long, trailing, bony tail was half the length of the entire reptile. In some types the tail was tipped by a paddle-like structure, which may have been a rudder. Pterodactyls were seen in the skies later, during the Jurassic and Cretaceous period. They

were also armed with teeth-filled beaks. But the tail was much shorter than in the rhamphorhynchs. Some pterodactyls had a body crest at the rear of the skull, to balance the beak.

Dimorphodon

Pterodaustro

Quetzalcoatlus   13m (43ft)

Ornithocheirus   *Pterodactylus*

Dimorphodon

Pterodaustro

Rhamphorhynchus

Quetzalcoatlus was the largest of all the pterosaurs. It probably soared in winds and hot-air thermals for most of the time, rather than actively flying. However, the smaller pterosaurs were powerful fliers, with strong muscles to flap their wings.

Pteranodon

Rhamphorhynchus

Rhamphorhynchus had a wing span of about 1m (3ft). It lived at the same time and in the same area as the tiny dinosaur Compsognathus.

HEADS, CRESTS AND BEAKS

One of the most distinctive features of various pterosaurs was the head, with its specialized beak for feeding and sometimes a bony crest. *Pterodaustro* had bristle-like 'teeth' to filter-feed upon tiny animals and plants in the water. *Pteranodon* had a long, curved beak for scooping fish and other creatures from the ocean. *Rhamphorhynchus* had a long, paddle-like bill, lined with sharp, interlocking teeth to grip slippery prey. *Dimorphodon* had a short, rounded beak, like the puffin. It may have fed on small fish.

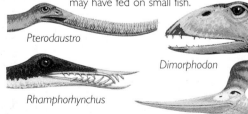

Pterodaustro

Dimorphodon

Rhamphorhynchus

Pteranodon

49

From Dinosaur to Bird

Sinosauropteryx

Did birds descend from dinosaurs? For years dinosaur experts have disagreed over this question. In a number of ways, birds are very

similar to the theropod or meat-eating group of dinosaurs – especially the smaller meat-eaters that walked and ran upright on their two hind legs. Some

dinosaurs, like *Compsognathus* or a small raptor, look especially like a bird, with a small, light frame and a long, pointed head. In fact, over twenty features are shared by this dinosaur and the early birds.

For many years, dinosaur experts argued that birds could not have descended from the dinosaurs, because birds have a wishbone, or

furcula. This is the V-shaped bone in the chest that braces the breastbone for added strength, to cope with the stresses of the powerful flying muscles. At the time, no dinosaurs had been discovered with a wishbone. However, in recent years several groups of theropod dinosaurs have been found to possess wishbones, including dromaeosaurs, oviraptors, troodontids and tyrannosaurs. With findings like these, many experts are now convinced of the link between birds and dinosaurs. They say that birds are, in effect, feathered dinosaurs.

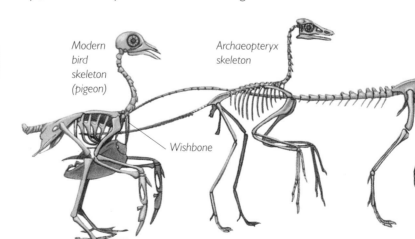

Modern bird skeleton (pigeon)

Wishbone

Archaeopteryx skeleton

Compsognathus skeleton

Like most modern-day birds, Compsognathus had a particularly light frame, with a long skull and jaws, and delicate limbs. Comparison of its skeleton with that of the prehistoric bird Archaeopteryx, and a modern-day bird, reveal many similarities.

50

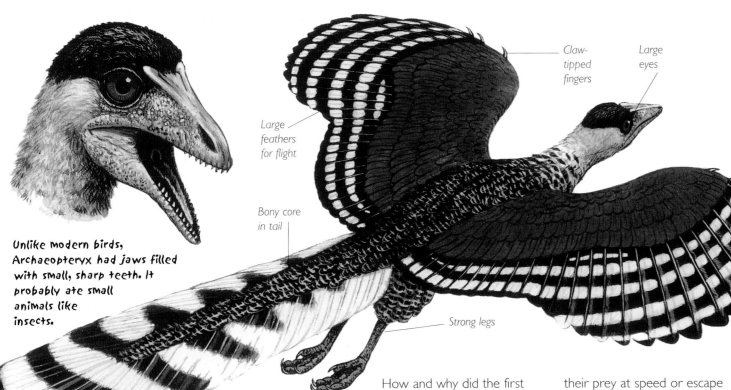

Unlike modern birds, Archaeopteryx had jaws filled with small, sharp teeth. It probably ate small animals like insects.

Large feathers for flight

Bony core in tail

Claw-tipped fingers

Large eyes

Strong legs

Archaeopteryx (left) is the earliest and best-known bird capable of flapping flight. But a number of recent fossil discoveries in China, like Sinosauropteryx (opposite) and Caudipteryx (below), have cast doubt on whether feathers evolved mainly for flight. The skin of these creatures was covered in downy, feather-like structures. Their function is not clear, though it may have been to do with temperature regulation.

The first known bird from good fossil remains is called *Archaeopteryx*, 'ancient wing'. Its first preserved skeleton was found in Germany in 1861. *Archaeopteryx* had features that were similar to both birds and reptiles. Its

reptile features included long jaws lined with teeth, claws at the ends of its wing fingers and a long, bony tail. Its bird-like features were long arms and fingers and, in particular, feathers. *Archaeopteryx* seems to be a midway stage – a previously missing link – between dinosaurs and birds.

How and why did the first birds learn to fly? Again, this topic is the subject of much argument. Perhaps they began to leap from the ground after low-flying insects, flapping their feathered arms to become air-borne. Or perhaps they descended from dinosaurs that lived in the trees. While hunting, these early dinosaurs may have leaped from the trees to the ground, to catch

their prey at speed or escape danger. Perhaps their scales developed into feathers, and over millions of years, they began to fly.

Caudipteryx is one of several dinosaurs with a covering of feathers and powerful legs. Its wings were not large or strong enough for flight, so feathers may have evolved for another reason.

Undersea Monsters

Life on land flourished during the dinosaur age, with many different species coming and going in the ever-changing environment. Life in the water was just as varied, with plentiful food sources, from fish and squid to shellfish. Many land creatures evolved (changed) to hunt in the waves and depths.

For many millions of years, sharks and squid successfully survived in the prehistoric seas. In fact, sharks were around well before the dinosaurs appeared. It is incredible to think that today, millions of years after the end of the dinosaur age, sharks are still prowling in the ocean. Some prehistoric sharks, like *Megalodon*, were even bigger, fiercer and more terrifying than the largest predatory shark today, the great white. But prehistoric sharks swam with a predator that was even bigger and more dangerous – a type of pliosaur (short-necked plesiosaur) called *Liopleurodon*. This was perhaps the largest predator that the world has ever known. It measured up to 25m (80ft) long – that's more than three times as long as the biggest great white shark! *Liopleurodon* rivalled the sperm whale, which is the biggest hunter in the seas today. The mouth alone of this monster was 3m (10ft) in length. Its entire head was an amazing 5m (16ft) long. It is hard so estimate the weight of this awesome creature, but it may have been more than 100 tons!

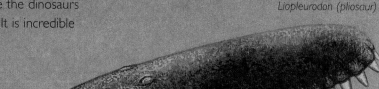

Liopleurodon (pliosaur)

Elasmosaurus (plesiosaur)

Archelon (turtle)

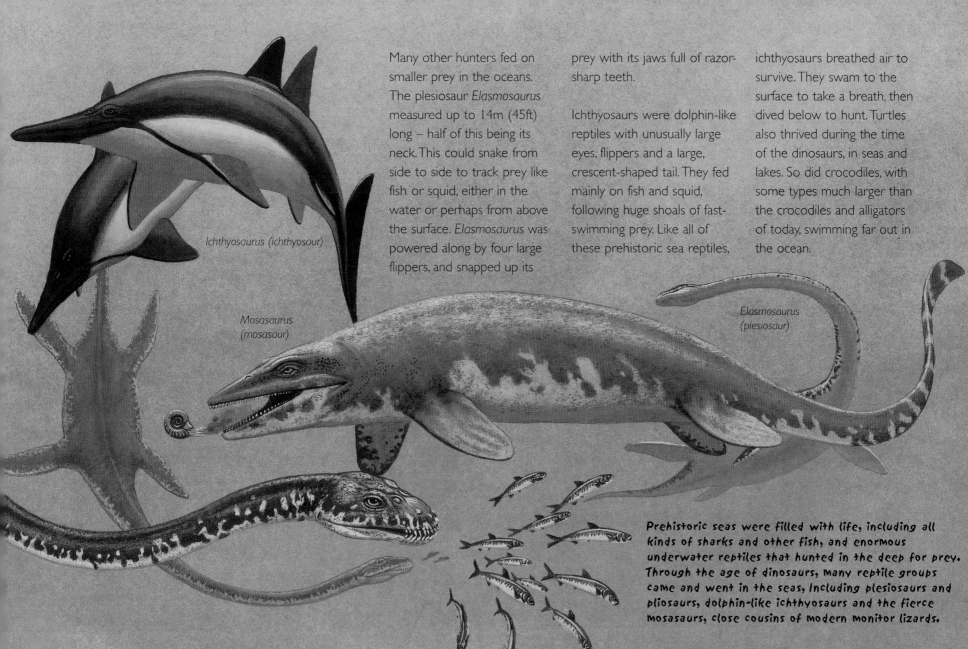

Many other hunters fed on smaller prey in the oceans. The plesiosaur *Elasmosaurus* measured up to 14m (45ft) long – half of this being its neck. This could snake from side to side to track prey like fish or squid, either in the water or perhaps from above the surface. *Elasmosaurus* was powered along by four large flippers, and snapped up its prey with its jaws full of razor-sharp teeth.

Ichthyosaurs were dolphin-like reptiles with unusually large eyes, flippers and a large, crescent-shaped tail. They fed mainly on fish and squid, following huge shoals of fast-swimming prey. Like all of these prehistoric sea reptiles, ichthyosaurs breathed air to survive. They swam to the surface to take a breath, then dived below to hunt. Turtles also thrived during the time of the dinosaurs, in seas and lakes. So did crocodiles, with some types much larger than the crocodiles and alligators of today, swimming far out in the ocean.

Ichthyosaurus (ichthyosaur)

Mosasaurus (mosasaur)

Elasmosaurus (plesiosaur)

Prehistoric seas were filled with life, including all kinds of sharks and other fish, and enormous underwater reptiles that hunted in the deep for prey. Through the age of dinosaurs, many reptile groups came and went in the seas, including plesiosaurs and pliosaurs, dolphin-like ichthyosaurs and the fierce mosasaurs, close cousins of modern monitor lizards.

Dangerous World

The dinosaurs dominated on Earth for longer than any other group of large animals. These incredible creatures adapted to an ever-changing world, evolving to survive in environments that wiped out many other forms of life. Through the dinosaur age, the world changed dramatically.

Land masses were ripped apart, and the world's climate experienced scorching temperatures and droughts, then cooler, wetter weather. All the time, the catastrophes that rock our world today hit the prehistoric planet, such as earthquakes and volcanic eruptions. Despite all of this, the dinosaurs survived for an incredible 165 million years – more than 30 times longer than humans have walked on the planet!

About 230 million years ago, at the dawn of the dinosaur age, the world was a very different place. Most of its surface was covered in water, and just one single landmass existed, but the climate was generally dry. Life was, as always, a struggle. The first dinosaurs were mainly fast-running predators that stood on their hind legs. This new breed of creature could withstand terrible droughts.

Dinosaur Facts

Tumours and growths found in fossil dinosaur bones prove that even these giant creatures fell victim to diseases such as cancers.

During volcanic eruptions toxic fumes could have suffocated any creature that came too close.

Like many modern animals, dinosaurs probably fought among themselves for mating rights and leadership.

Accidents also could prove dangerous for dinosaurs. Broken bones and fractured limbs would make hunting, or running away, impossible.

About 200 million years ago the Earth became wetter towards the poles, marking the birth of the Jurassic period. Lush vegetation began to grow and it was during this time that the giant plant-eating and meat-eating dinosaurs started to appear. But it was 135 million years later, towards the end of the Cretaceous period, that further hazards began to threaten the dinosaur world.

The earth's landscape went through dramatic changes. Huge volcanic eruptions took place, building up some of the landscapes that we see in the world today. The volcanoes also threw enormous amounts of carbon dioxide and acid into the air, to be carried around the world by winds. The overheated Earth may have been pelted with acid rain, which destroyed the protective ozone layer. Survival for the dinosaurs during this time of violent change would have been tough, and it has even been suggested that these changes may have contributed to their extinction.

Wandering Parasaurolophus (opposite) and migrating Centrosaurus (left) faced many dangers, as they navigated powerful rivers to reach breeding or feeding grounds. Volcanic eruptions with hot ash and choking fumes, flash floods and storms could wipe out entire herds.

End of the Dinosaurs

The giant asteroid that hit the Earth about 66 million years ago would have caused terrible earthquakes and enormous tidal waves all over the world.

Scientists think that the asteroid which contributed to the dinosaurs' extinction must have been at least 10km (6 miles) wide.

A vast crater was found in the Gulf of Mexico in 1991, supporting the asteroid theory.

From studying fossils, dinosaur hunters believe that dinosaur numbers began to decrease long before their extinction, perhaps from 80–75 million years ago.

Why did the dinosaurs die out? There are many different theories, including asteroid impact, volcanic activity and climate change, but no single idea has been accepted as the absolute answer. We cannot know for sure, of course, why these great reptiles became extinct. But we can make some good guesses by looking at the dramatic events and changes that occurred towards the end of their time on Earth.

Although the dinosaurs died out about 66 million years ago, not all life on Earth was destroyed. Many kinds of animals and plants survived.

Also, the extinction event that wiped out dinosaurs and others was not the only one. A much more serious mass extinction occurred some 185 million years earlier, at the end of the Permian period, even before the first dinosaurs walked the Earth. During this earlier catastrophe, over nine-tenths of life-forms on our planet were destroyed – in fact, life in many areas virtually came to an end.

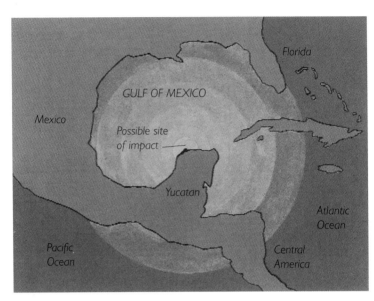

An enormous crater has been discovered in the Earth's crust just off the coast of Mexico. It could be the crater made by a huge meteorite or asteroid (a large rock that travels through space). The crater, called Chicxulub, is now buried under many metres/feet of sea-bed mud.

The land surface of Earth is pock-marked by many craters, caused by meteorites that have hit the Earth in the past. A similar event about 66 million years ago may have led to the extinction of the dinosaurs.

Although the mass extinction 66 million years ago saw the death of the dinosaurs, various creatures did survive. Mammals, birds, frogs and salamanders, insects and some water-living creatures lived on. What is even more puzzling is that while dinosaurs and several other reptile groups disappeared – including pterosaurs and ichthyosaurs – crocodiles, turtles, lizards and others survived. Why did some reptiles live, yet others did not?

Some scientists believe that smaller, scavenging animals like the mammals survived because the great extinction was brought about by the collision of a giant asteroid with Earth. An enormous crater (hole) in the Earth's crust has been found just off the Gulf of Mexico. It may have been the site at which the asteroid hit the Earth. A large asteroid collision would have caused an incredible explosion, sending a cloud of dust and rocks into the Earth's

atmosphere. The cloud would have blocked out the sunlight for at least three months, destroying virtually all plant-life. The plant-eating dinosaurs' sourse of food would have vanished. As herds of plant-eaters began to die, the food source of the meat-eaters would have disappeared too. Only smaller scavengers would have been able to find food, in the form of millions of huge carcasses.

It may well have been a combination of events that finally killed off the dinosaurs – rapid climate change and enormous volcanic eruptions, plus the terrible asteroid collision. All would have had

a catastrophic effect upon the dinosaurs, leading to the final sudden decline of the most successful group of large animals that ever lived.

SURVIVORS

A number of creatures survived the catastrophe that wiped out the dinosaurs. Among these were birds, mammals, some sea creatures and insects. It is possible that these creatures survived because they were able to endure the difficult climate and environmental changes that may have killed the dinosaurs.

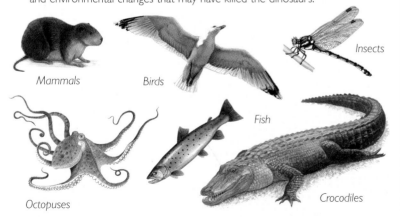

Mammals

Birds

Insects

Octopuses

Fish

Crocodiles

Dinosaurs Again?

Exciting films like the *Jurassic Park* series have brought dinosaurs 'back to life' through their incredibly realistic computer-generated images. The *Jurassic Park* story itself tells of dinosaurs recreated by advanced genetic engineering, using tiny strands of DNA from the blood of a fossilized mosquito! However exciting an idea this may

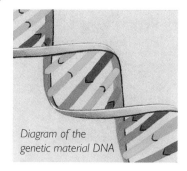

Diagram of the genetic material DNA

be, it is very unlikely that dinosaurs will ever be reborn in our lifetimes.

Since the earliest discoveries of dinosaur fossils, people have been fascinated by these magnificent creatures, and have flocked to see their reconstructions. In the 1850s, huge crowds of people

journeyed to the exhibition of life-sized dinosaur models at Crystal Palace, London. Although these bulky and heavy-limbed models were thought to be correct at the time, we now know that most dinosaurs were more light-boned and agile creatures, rather than clumsy, lumbering great lizards.

Modern-day models are much more realistic and closer to the actual appearance of these prehistoric creatures, although various doubts remain and new ideas constantly appear.

Dinosaur reconstruction is a long and painstaking process in which the fossils are slotted together, piece by piece, like a big jigsaw puzzle.

Fossil of an insect in amber

In the adventure film Jurassic Park, dinosaurs are grown from the genetic instructions in DNA from their blood, trapped inside a perfectly preserved mosquito. Tiny, isolated fragments of prehistoric DNA have been found in fossil leaves and insects, but by no means enough to even begin any attempts at recreation.

The first full-sized models of dinosaurs were displayed at Crystal Palace, London, in 1854. Although very different from the same dinosaurs reconstructed today, the life-like, life-sized beasts astounded and fascinated all who saw them. From that time, dinosaurs have been a magnet for young and old alike.

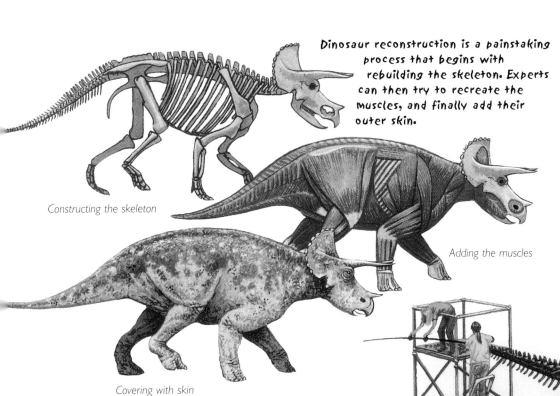

Dinosaur reconstruction is a painstaking process that begins with rebuilding the skeleton. Experts can then try to recreate the muscles, and finally add their outer skin.

Constructing the skeleton

Adding the muscles

Covering with skin

BRINGING DINOSAURS BACK TO LIFE

Computer programs have helped to create incredibly life-like dinosaurs and other long-dead animals, for the large and small screen. By using a combination of models, robotics, stop-motion animation, computer graphics and computer-aided animation, film-makers can attempt to show what dinosaurs looked like, and how they moved, hunted and courted. They rely heavily on advice from experts on living creatures.

Natural history museums have restored many dinosaur skeletons and life-sized models. The 'fossils' on display are usually lightweight plastic or glass-fibre copies. The real ones are solid rock, very heavy, and often rather delicate and extremely valuable.

Programming the robotics

Putting together the basic skeleton

It is exceptionally rare to find a dinosaur skeleton intact, and important pieces of bones, teeth, horns, claws and other parts are often missing. It is only by studying the tiny details of many fossils, as well as looking at modern animals such as crocodiles and birds, that experts can rebuild these prehistoric giants.

Even though we cannot bring dinosaurs back to life, model-makers and film-makers have been able to design animated versions. By studying the shape, body structure and movements of modern-day animals, we can make a guess about dinosaur coloration, and how they walked and ran across their world.

59

Dinosaurs Today

Dinosaurs are all around us in the world today – in the shape of birds! At least, this is what many dinosaur experts agree. If birds did descend directly from smallish meat-eating dinosaurs, such as raptors, they are the only creatures which did so, and which are still alive today. Unlike the flying reptiles of the prehistoric age, birds seemed able to adapt to the conditions that caused and followed the mass extinction of the dinosaurs. Perhaps their size was a factor in their survival, because larger flying creatures like the pterosaurs died out with the dinosaurs. It is remarkable to think that the birds we see today are probably our closest links with the giant reptiles that ruled the planet for so long.

Komodo dragon

Tuatara

Common iguana

Modern-day lizards may seem like close relations of dinosaurs. But there are many differences, including their limb structure. Lizards have a sprawling posture.

Dinosaur Facts

The tuatara is a very rare reptile resembling a lizard, that lives in New Zealand. Like some dinosaurs, it has a row of pointed spikes along its back.

The Komodo dragon is the biggest lizard in the world, and looks like a modern-day dinosaur. But lizards, even though they are reptiles, are not especially close cousins of dinosaurs.

Mammals survived through almost the whole of the dinosaur age - and ever since.

Of the reptiles alive today, the closest relatives to dinosaurs are the crocodiles.

Although not easily recognized as direct descendants of the dinosaurs, it is now believed that birds are indeed their closest living relatives.

Robin

Barn owl

Swallow

Heron

Ostrich

Cockerel

Penguin

Swan

Crocodiles, alligators and caimans – together known as crocodilians – are perhaps the next-closest living relatives of dinosaurs. They still lurk in fresh and salt water around the world. Crocodiles look remarkably similar to some prehistoric sea reptiles, and are certainly one of the oldest large animal groups on Earth.

Mammals, too, survived from the time of the dinosaurs. During the Permian period, before the dinosaurs arrived to rule the land, the group known as mammal-like reptiles were the dominant land creatures. As the dinosaurs flourished in the Mesozoic era, these mammal-like reptiles gave rise to the true mammals that are so familiar in all corners of the world.

One group of mammal-like reptiles was the cynodonts. They were very similar to modern-day mammals. Some types resembled dogs, and they form a link between the mammal-like reptiles and true mammals.

For the millions of years that dinosaurs ruled the land, small mammals survived by hiding in the undergrowth and scurrying around at night. Only when the dinosaurs were wiped out about 66 million years ago, did mammals truly begin to flourish.

The death of the dinosaurs and other large reptiles left the land, sky and sea less crowded. Mammals and birds evolved quickly to fill the new opportunities for food, living space and shelter. In turn this led, some 60 million years later, to the first types of humans on Earth. Human beings owe a great deal to the mass extinction of the dinosaurs. If it had never taken place, we ourselves may never have walked the Earth!

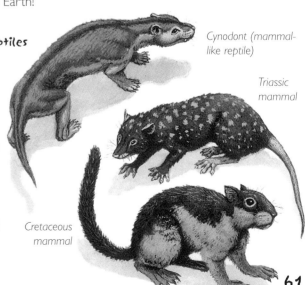

As in dinosaur times, various types of mammal meat-eaters have been and gone. Smilodon was a sabre-tooth cat that preyed on mammoths, deer and bison in North America. Its remains have been found preserved in natural tar pits in what is now California, USA.

Mammoths are ancient cousins of today's elephants. They died out only some 10,000 years ago, as the great Ice Age ended.

Woolly mammoths

Mammal-like reptiles of the early Triassic period gave way to the first true mammals later in that period. The Cretaceous saw newer groups of mammals, although they were still small in size.

Cynodont (mammal-like reptile)

Triassic mammal

Cretaceous mammal

61

Glossary

Acid rain — rain turned to weak acid by gases from volcanoes or pollution.

Asteroid — a mass of rock that moves through space, sometimes entering a planet's atmosphere to collide with its surface.

Cannibal — a creature that feeds upon its own species.

Carnivore — a meat-eating animal. Carnivores hunt live prey, or feed off the remains of an already dead animal.

Co-dependence — a situation in which two or more creatures depend upon each other for their survival.

Co-existence — a situation in which two or more creatures live side-by-side in the same environment.

Cold-blooded — (of) an animal whose body temperature is controlled by its surroundings.

Computer-generated — created by a computer program.

Courtship — the way in which a male and female animal behave before mating.

Dinosaur — a land-living reptile that existed over 66 million years ago.

DNA — deoxyribonucleic acid, a material that is found in all living things. DNA carries the characteristics of an animal or plant species, which are passed on through each generation.

Embryo — the name given to a developing baby while still inside an egg, or the mother's womb.

Evolution — the way in which an animal or plant species changes over a period of time, often in response to changes in its environment.

Extinction — the dying out of an entire species of animal or plant.

Fossil — the (usually petrified) remains of part of a prehistoric plant or animal, such as a shell, tooth or a bone.

Gastrolith — a smooth stone that is swallowed by an animal to help it grind up food inside its stomach.

Genetic engineering — the way in which DNA is used to change or recreate a living organism.

Hatchling — a young animal that has recently hatched from its egg.

Herbivore — a plant-eating animal.

Land mass — a large, continuous area of land not divided by water.

Ligament — a long, tough band of material that joins bone and muscle.

Migration — to move from one area to another. Many animals migrate to find food or a better environment, or to breed.

Organism — any living animal or plant.

Ozone layer — an area of atmosphere above Earth that protects it from the harmful rays of the sun.

Palaeontologist — someone who studies fossils to find out about ancient forms of life.

Parasite — something that feeds off another living organism for its survival.

Predator — a flesh-eating animal that hunts down other living animals for food.

Prehistoric — the period of time before humans began to record their existence in writing.

Reproduction — the way in which animals and other organisms make babies.

Reptile — a cold-blooded animal that is usually covered in scales and reproduces by laying eggs.

Sauropod — a group of huge, plant-eating dinosaurs that walked on all four legs. Sauropods had extremely long necks and tails.

Species — a type of animal or plant that share the same physical characteristics.

Theropod — a flesh-eating dinosaur that moved about on its two hind legs.

Warm-blooded — (of) an animal whose body temperature stays the same regardless of its surroundings.

Index